Political Awakening in Jammu Region

Political Awakening in Jammu Region

Dr. Sandhya Dhar

KALPAZ

First Published, 2019

Published by

Kalpaz Publications
C-30, Satyawati Nagar,
Delhi – 110052
Ph.: 011-47034999, 9811692060
www.kalpazpublications.com
E-mail: kalpaz@hotmail.com

Printed at: G. Print Process, Delhi

Cataloging in Publication Data—DK
Courtesy: D.K. Agencies (P) Ltd. <docinfo@dkagencies.com>

Dhar, Sandhya, author.
Political awakening in Jammu region : papers presented in seminars, conferences / Dr. Sandhya Dhar.
pages cm
Includes bibliographical references.
ISBN 9789353240295

1. Jammu (India : Region)—Politics and government—20th century. 2. Social movements—India—Jammu (Region)—History—20th century. I. Title.

LCC DS485.K26D43 2018 | DDC 954.6 23

Dedicated

to

The Loving

Memories of

My Parents and Brother

Contents

Acknowledgements

I will always be remaining greatful to my father Late Mohan Lal Dhar, Late Meera Dhar my mother and Late Sanjay Dhar my brother who have inspired me. Their fond and loving memories will always remain in my heart. It is with their blessings I have been able to complete this book successfully.

Greateful to the, J.N.U. Library, Delhi; I.G.N.O.U. Acknowledgements Library, Delhi. Ranbir Library, Jammu Central Library, Jammu University; Department Library of History Department.Without their co-operation, it would not have been possible for me to complete this work.

Preface

The people's awakening throughout the world is because of socio-economic and political factors. The dawn of 20th century brought awakening and political consciousness in Jammu region. This awakening was because of economic exploitation, social mal-adjustment and political domination which gave rise to a vigorious battle for self-identification of the people of Jammu region.

A number of books have come out recently regarding Jammu &Kashmir, they deal mainly with partition, Kashmir Struggle, Kashmir Development, Kashmir Awakening etc. but nothing has been written on Jammu's struggle, Jammu's awakening etc. Only off hand and tangential remarks on this subject in their writings.

So, to find out the importance of this subject, I presented a number of papers in Saminars, conferences, Indian History Congress and Punjab History Conference etc.

However the work is primarily based on National Archive records, J&K State Archives, Jammu. Government Publications, Census Reports, Journals, Dissertations, Newspapers and books.

My hartiest thanks to the staff of the State Archive of Jammu & Kashmir, Jammu, Central Liberary Jammu University, Delhi National Archive, New Delhi.

Introduction

The state of Jammu and Kashmir in its present form came into being on 16th March 1846 when the British handed over the state to Maharaja Gulab Singh through the treaty of Amritsar. The three regions Kashmir, Jammu and Laddakh came under the rule of Gulab Singh, the Hindu Dogra Ruler. The three regions havings distinct cultures, languages, ethnic and socio-psychological characteristics were brought under one administrative unit for the first time under aforesaid treaty.[1]

The state of Jammu and Kashmir occupies a position of great strategic importance in the north-west of India.[2] It is separated from the rest of the country by mountainous and uneven terrain.[3] A prominent feature of the state is its heterogeneous composition, i.e., geographically, culturally and religion-wise. Geographically, it is divided into four natural divisions. The southern plains, the mountainous region, the middle track of Himalayas and the far-off Himalayan region.[4]

The first region consists of plains bordering the Punjab and the broken mass of the foothills known locally as Kandi areas[5]. On account of being its mostly strong and arid, cultivation here is scanty, scattered and wholly dependent on rain. The whole of Jammu district and part of Kathua fall into this region. Rest of the Jammu province, i.e. district of Udhampur, Poonch, Doda, and part of Kathua fall in the outer hill region. It consists of low hills laying roughly to the south of Pir Panchal range which separates two provinces of Jammu and Kashmir.[6] Except in the fertile valleys formed by the river and its tributaries, cultivation is scare and scattered and is done on small patches.[7] The middle-track of Himalayas, the third geographical region of the state is known as the Kashmir valley.[8] The region has a rich alluvial soil and paddy and fruits are the main produces of the region. The rest of the state consists almost entirely of snow-capped mountains, with plateaus and glaciers, rocky river valleys and wastes.[9] At present, it comprises of Kargil and Leh divisions of frontier district of Laddakh. The whole of the area is dry and almost rainless. The cultivation of barley maize and millets is, however, undertaken in this region with the help of irrigation from small canals known as "Kuhls" which are fed by melting snow.[10]

Jammu Under a Dogra Rule

In the beginning of the twentieth century, the state was being ruled by Maharaja Pratap Singh (1885 - 1925 AD) who had succeeded his father, Maharaja Ranbir Singh on 12th September, 1885.[11] Soon after his accession, the relation between the Maharaja and the British Indian Government became strained. In 1889, Lord Lansdowne deprived the Maharaja of his political power on account of false charges of mal-administration.[12] A four-member council headed by Raja Amar Singh, brother of Maharaja Pratap Singh, was constituted to carry on the administration of the State.[13] However, in 1891, Lord Lansdowne paid a visit to Kashmir, and a new Council was constituted with Maharaja Pratap Singh as its President and Raja Amar Singh as Vice-president. Four other members were also nominated to this council.[14] The Council was guided by the advice of the British Resident in Kashmir in all matters of importance.[15] In 1905, the Council was abolished and its powers were restored to Maharaja himself,[16] assisted by the Chief Minister, Raja Amar Singh and ministers in-charge of the Revenue and

Judicial and Home Departments.[17] However, the Maharaja's powers, especially in financial matters, were subject to manifold restrictions.

The annual budget had to be prepared in consultation with the British Resident in Kashmir, and to incur expenditure not provided for in the budget, previous approval of the Resident had to be sought. Thus, the Resident exercised full financial control over the state exchequer.[18] However, these restrictions were gradually relaxed and the Maharaja was granted full administrative powers, in March 1921.[19]

In 1901, Jammu region was divided into four districts, Jammu, Udhampur, Bhimber, Jasrota and two main feudatory Jagirs, Bhaderwah and Poonch.[20] The rulers of these Jagirs were feudatories to the Maharaja and their relationship was defined by Ranbir family code [Dustur-ul-Amal), which was revised by Maharaja Pratap Singh on 25th March, 1893.[21] This system continued till 1928 when a revised 'Patta' was issued to govern the relation between the Maharaja and the Raja of Poonch, according to which the latter was to abide by and follow without demure, the advice and direction of the former in all important matters. During the decade 1901-1911, district Bhimber was abolished and two new districts[22] of Mirpur and Reasi were constituted in its place. Mirpur district included the tehsils of Mirpur, Bhimber and Kotli while the tehsils of Reasi and Rampur-Rajouri constituted the district of Reasi.[23] After partition, the Doda district was carved out of Udhampur district in 1948, with this change Reasi lost its district status and became a tehsil headquarter in Udhampur district. At the same time, Poonch district was carved out from the territories of Poonch jagir and Rampur-Rajouri, which was previously a part of Reasi District. However, in 1968, Rajouri was given the status of district. During the year 2007, the state was again reorganized by creating eight more districts. Of these four are in Kashmir Province and four in Jammu province. In Jammu, the four districts are Samba, Kishtwar, Ramban and Reasi.

Jammu region, one of the constituents of Jammu and Kashmir state lies between 32°-15' to 33°-30' North Latitude and 74° to 76°-15' East Longitude.[24] The province was surrounded by Chamba and Kangra in the east, by Jhelum district in the west by Gujarat district in the south-west, and Sialkot and Gurdaspur district of the undivided Punjab in the south, while the Pir Panjal separated it from Kashmir, in the north.[25]

In 1901, the area of Jammu province was 12,378 sq miles.[26] After 1947, some parts of Poonch and the major portion of Mirpur district came under the illegal possession of Pakistan, and the area of the province shrank to 10,073.1 sq. miles.[27] In terms of area, Jammu region was the second largest constituent of the state.

The flat sub-mountain tract of Jammu region[28] has the soil of tarai lands of the east. It is alluvial in nature varying from loam to sandy loom. Phosphate and potash contents of the soil are fairly good, but nitrogen content is lesser. Being fertile, this plain tract of the province shares the advantages of the Punjab plains.[29]

Arid kandi is composed of ferruginous clay intermixed with soil and stone. Parched kandi tracts are found in the tehsils of Kathua, Hiranagar, Samba, Akhnoor and in some parts of Jammu and Rajouri. This kind of soil is also found in Bhimber and Mirpur tehsils. Being water bearing horizon found at great depth, 50 to 300 feet, this tract is unsuited for digging wells.[30]

Corresponding to two natural divisions there are two different climatic zones in the region. The plain and Kandi tracts experience the tropical heat of the Punjab and here the maximum temperature in 1931, stood at 45.7 centigrade and the minimum at 2.5 centigrade.[31] Other parts of the region situated comparatively on higher elevations in the outer hills, experience sub-tropical temperature. However, along the Pir-Panchal range one experiences the climate of temperate zone of Kashmir.[32] One can enjoy salubrious climate at Bhaderwah, Kishtwar and Poonch.[33] While in Jammu scorching heat is experienced in June.

In Jammu region only Chenab, Ravi and Poonch river are snow fed rivers carrying greater amount of water than the rest of the rivers throughout the year. Other rivers are Ujh, Jhelum and Besanlis Tawi.[34]

Because of geographic determinants, crop pattern in this region differs from region to region. The sub mountain tract of the region below 2,000 feet, yields all the usual crops of the Punjab, viz., wheat, barley, gram Sarshaf (rape) in Rabi (spring) and maize, millet, pulses, cotton, rice and sugarcane in Kharif (autumn).[35] Most of the land especially in kandi and outer hills are ek fasli (yielding only a single crop in a year due to lack of artificial irrigation facilities.[36]

Jammu region accounted for more than 53 per cent of the (15,21,307 persons) population of the state in 1901, and 56.60 per cent (15,97,865 persons) in 1911. The rate of increase in the population of the region, during the decade (1901-1911) was 5.3 per cent as against 8.7 percent in the whole state.[37] The cause of low increase of population, in comparison to the whole state, were poor harvests and visitations of plague and malaria in the lower tracts of the region, where these epidemics caused heavy mortality.[38]

In 1901, out of population of 10,000 in the province the Muslim numbered 5,762, Hindus 4,116, Sikhs 86, Buddhists 32, Jains three and Christian one.[39] In 1911, the numbers of Muslims 5,966, Hindus 3,921, Sikhs 104, Christians four, Buddhists three and Jains two. From these figures it is quite evident that the Sikhs and Christians were adding to their number rapidly. Both these communities were attracting large number of persons to their fold through proselytisation in spite of the opposition of the orthodox people.[40]

Occupation soil exploitation in one form or the other was the most important economic activity of the province. In the beginning of the twentieth century more than three-fourth of the population was exclusively dependent on agriculture and its allied pursuits.[41] Absence of satisfactory means of communication and the hilly terrain of the province retarded the growth of trade and industry. Hence, economically the province compared unfavorably with the Punjab and other parts of northern India.[42] The following statistics will show the relative importance of the main occupations in the economy of the people of this province.[43]

In the field of education, Jammu region was the most backward regions of India. This was due to the scattered population, which meant long distance between local points of education and their habitation and very limited schooling facilities. To achieve the goal of education for all was not an easy task, particularly in a traditional society like the one in the Jammu region where; Pari Patti Gali Taratti; Hoi Vage Tubra Khage (meaning education brings his ruins, it is by ploughing that bread can be had).[44] Lack of means of communication the general indifference of the people and very limited schooling facilities.[45] Moreover, female education was altogether neglected expected in a few progressive families, parents were generally opposed to girls education.[46]

In the beginning of the twentieth century the literacy rate was very low. According to the census report of 1921 only 27 persons out of every 1.000 were literate in this region. The proportion of literate among the males of this province in 1921 was 47, while among females it was only four.[47] The proportion of English knowing persons in this region in 1921 was still lower. It was only 4.4 per thousand among males and per thousand among females.[48]

However, during the decade 1921-1931 condition improved considerably and the level of literacy in the province rose to 49 per thousand in 1931. Among males the proportion had gone upto eighty two and among females up to ten per thousand.[49] By the year 1941, the proportion of literates per thousand of population in this region had risen to seventy four,[50] as against seventy in Kashmir region and thirty one in frontier districts, excluding Gilgit Agency.[51] With the expansion of schools and colleges during the following two decades, particularly after the forties, literacy level region rose up to 14.6 per cent in 1961.[52]

From 1889-1946 in Jammu, there was only one college, 15 high schools, 43 middle schools, 49 primary schools and four teachers' training schools, etc.[53]

As described above, there was no road fit for wheeled traffic which could link the interior of the region. Sanction to the construction of Jammu-Udhampur cart Road was accorded by 1904-1905.[54] Lining work of Nandini Tunnel, 16 miles this road, was executed in 1910-11.[55] Construction of the Banihal card completed as late as in 1922, to whom we called J.V. (Jehlum valley) tunnel. The isolation of the province was partly shaken when Jammu-Sialkot ,the first railway line in the state commence in1890.[56]

References

1. Pannikar K.M., Founding of Kashmir State London, 1930, p. 39.
2. Mountainous State of J & K almost centrally located in the continent of Asia, in the neighbourhood of Pamir, the roof the world, is popularly termed as the Jewel Decked crown of India. It is bounded by China in the north-west and Pakistan in the west. It is only in the south that it is linked with rest of Indian union. Projected deep into the heart of Asia, Jammu and Kashmir, a component state of Indian union covers an area of 86,023 Sq Kms. extending from 32°17'N to 37°5'N longitude and 72'40'E to 80030'E latitude. The ceasefire agreement of 1 st January, 1949 with Pakistan left 84,112 Sq Kms. of area in control of Pakistan. The areas included Giligat, Skardu, Magafrabed, a large part of Poonch Jagir, Mirpur district and its adjoining areas. Sudden aggression China in 1962 captured an area of 41,500 Sq Kms.

3. State of J & K occupies, the sixth place in respect of area and sixteenth in respect of population of India.
4. Gupta, N.S., and Singh Amarjit, Agricultural Development of states in India: Jammu and Kashmir, Vol.1, Seema, New Delhi, 1979, p. 12.
5. Average height of this region is about 2,000 ft above sea level. The river Chenab flows through it.
6. A large part of this areas laying between 2,000 to 4,000 feet above sea level.The river Chenab passes through this area also.
7. Gupta, N.S., and Amarjit Singh, op. cit. N. 3, pp. 13-14.
8. The river Jhelum with its tributaries, pursuing a zigzag course, flows through the whole length of Valley, bisecting it into almost two halves. The average height of the Valley is 5,500 feet above sea level, while mountains surrounding it average 12,000 feet with a dip to about 9,000 feet at Banihal Pass.
9. The Indus is the main river of the region. There are a number of mountains over 2,000 feet in height.
10. Due to its topography and scarcity of cultivable land, the distribution of population is most uneven in the state, i.e., Srinagar, Anantnag, Baramulla and Jammu with about 13.7 per cent of total area, contain about 69 per cent of total population.
11. G.O.I F.D Progs. Nov. 1912, No. 62/Deposit-I: Crown films No. 294 (N A.I.) see Fraser's note regarding the rule of His Highness the Maharaja Sir Pratap Singh.
12. Ibid, Saraf, Mulkh Raj, Jammu and Kashmir Encyclopaedia, 1846-1946, Urdu, 1946, p. 113. Nargis, Narsingh Dass, Tarikh Dogra Desh, (Urdu), Jammu, 1967, pp. 698-701.
13. Ibid, p. 700. Saraf Mulkh Raj, op. cit.,p. 113.Members of the council were:- Raja Amar Singh(President), Raja Ram Singh (Commander-in-Chief ofArmy), Rai Bhadur Pandit Suraj Kaul (RevenueMember) and Rai Bhadur Pandit Bhag Ram (Judicial Member).

    (i) G.O.I., F.D. Progs. Nov. 1912, No. 62/Deposit-I: Crown films No. 294; (if) Nargis, op. tit., p. 700.
14. Saraf, Mulkh Raj, op. cit., p. 116.
15. G.O.L, F.D. Progs. Nov. 1904, No. 330/Intl-B.
16. G.O.I., P.D., Progs. Nov. 1912, No. 62/Desposit-I; Crown film No. 294; G.O.I., F.P.D., Progs. July 1919, Nos. 70-74/Secret-Intl: Crown film No. 293; G.O.I., F.P.D., Progs. March 1921,

Nos. 1-17/Secret-I; Crown Film No. 292; Nove, Arthur, Thirty Years in Kashmir. London, 1913, p. 48.

17. I.G.I., 1909, p. 72. Sufi, G.M.D., Kashmir, Vol. II, 1949, pp. 807, 815.
18. G.O.I., F.P.D., Progs. March 1914, Nos 1-2/Secret-I: Crown film No. 293 (N.A.I.).
19. G.O.I.,F.P.D., Progs. March 1921, Nos. 1-17/Secret-I; Crown Film No. 292; G.O.I., F.P.D., File No. 180-Pol. (Secret) of 1923, pp. 3-16; Crown film No. 1291.

    Saraf, Mulkh Raj, Op. cit., PP. 117, 148 to 151; Nargis, op. cit, p. 702.
20. Census 1901, K. Part 1, p. XII (Introduction), Ibid, Part II, p. 1.
21. G.O.I., ED. Progs, Oct. 1902, NOSL 111-115, and GO.L, P.P.D., File No. 289. Provisions of Dustur-ul-AmaV revised by Maharaja Prop Singh were, I." Annual tribute of Rs. 233.5 annas. 4 Pices., viz., the amount fixed in Sir Frederick Currie's Robbar, dated the 12 May, 1948, can be claimed by His Highness the Maharaja.
22. G.O.I., P.D., File No. 579-P/Sec of 1936, p. 1, and crown Film No. 3(B)P/Sec of 1940, pp 1-3, and crown film No. 288 (N.A.9).
23. Census 1911. K. Part 1. p. 6.

    Census 1931, J&K Part 1. pp. 2. 3.4. A Report on economic and industrial Survey of the State of Jammu and Kashmir. 1935, 39, 9. J&K. Pub. p. 2-3. 24. Sharma, Baldev, "Entomological Survey of Jammu Region," unpublished thesis, Jammu University. Deptt. of Bio - Science, 1975, p. 9.
25. See Map, Census 1931, K. Part-I.
26. Ibid., p. 6.
27. Census 1961, Vol. VI, J&K, Part IX, p. 36. Ibid, Vol. VI, J&K Part I-A (i), p. 150.
28. Census 1901K. Part. l,p. I; Census 191 IK. Part l,p. II; Census 1921K, Part 1, p. 4; Census J93JK, Part 1, p. 7; Census 1941K, Part 1, p. 72.

    Census 296i, Vol. VI, J&K, Part IX, p. 36. The figures of areas, taken from the census of 1901 are not reliable as these were based on Drew's estimate in Jammu and Kashmir territories, 1875. No survey-had been conducted in the beginning of twentieth century and even the settlement operations were in their preliminary stage, to arrive at the correct figures of area.

In the census of 1911, the superintendent in-charge made strenuous efforts to arrive at the correct figures of area. His estimate was based on the information supplied by the survey of India. Thus, he achieved partial success. The figures of area in the census of 1921 were again obtained from the survey of India, but the estimate was not wholly reliable because of the incomplete information with regard to Udhampur district. Only the census of 1931 gives the correct information of area which was based on the correct estimates, supplied by the survey Department of India (Census 1931, J & K Part I, P. 7).

29. Census 1931, J & K Part I, p. 7.
30. *Ibid.,* p. 7.
31. *Ibid.,* p. 10.
32. Census 1961, Vol. VI. VI, J & K Part I-A (i), D 150; Saraf, Mulkh Raj, Jammu and Kashmir Guids, 1969, p. 31. After the tribal raids in 1947 the tehsils of Bagh and Pleadari, some parts of tehsils Handi, Mendhar, Rajouri and Major portion of Mirpur district fell on the other side of ceasefire line. This necessitated for the territorial readjustment of districts, Poonch, a feudatory Jagir under the sovereignty of Maharaja of Jammu and Kashmir upto 1947, was constituted of full-fledged district with residual portions of tehsil Haveli, Mendhar, Rajouri and parts of Kotli tehsil, left on this side of ceasefire line tehsil Reasi was transferred to Udhampur district and Doda was created a separate district, tabbing Bhaderwah Doda, Kishtwar and Ramban tehsils of Udhampur district.
33. Census 1961, Vol. VI, J & K Part I-A (i), p,147.
34. *Ibid.*
35. Census 1921, K. Parti, p. 2.

    Census 1931, J&K Part I, pp. 2, 3, 4. Report on Economic and Industrial Survey of the State of Jammu and Kashmir 1938-39, G. J & K, Pub., pp. 2-3.
36. Census 1931, J&K Part I, p. 2. A handbook of Jammu and Kashmir State, 1945, G. J&K Pub., p. 1.
37. Census 1921, K. Part I, p. 2.
38. Randhawa, M.S., Framers of India, Vol. I, 1959, p. 198, and Bose, S.C., Geopgraphy of the Himalayas, 1972, p. 125.
39. Douie, Sir James, The Punjab, North-West Frontier Province and 14 Kashmir 1916, p. 3D and Adm. Report., 1997-98 (1940-41 A.D.), p. 2.

40. Census 1961, Vol. Part VI, No. 21, p. 1 and Confidential Gazetteer of Kashmir and Laddakh, 1980, reprint 1974 pp. 287-288 and Randhawa, M.S, op. cit, p. 198.
41. Census 1901, K. Part II, p. 7; Census 1911, K. Part II, p. 2; Census 1921, K. Part I, p. 35. Figures of percentage have been worked out on the basis of census data of 1901 and 1911.
42. Census 1931, J&K, Part 1, pp. 20-21.

    G.O.I., F.D.Progs. Nov. 1902 Nos. 1-21 Incl./B.
43. Census 1901, K. Part I, p. 34 and Part II Tab. VI, pp. 2, and census 1911 K, Part-I, pp. 88-107, and Adm. Report J&K, S. 1968, P. I. (Figures of percentage worked out on the basis of census data).
42. Census 1911, K. Parti, pp. 96-108. Census 1921, K. Part I, pp. 66-67.
45. Census 1901,K. Part I, p. 104. Census 1921, K. Part I, p. 226.
46. Figures of percentage calculated on the basis of census data of 1901 and 1911. For detail see Census 1901, op. cit.,pp 104-108 and Census 1911, op. cit., p. 243.

    Census 1901, K. Part I, p. 80. Census 1911, K. Parti, p. 201.
47. Binglay, Capt. A.H., Dogras, 1899, pp. 18-25, and I.G.I, Vol. XV, 1908, pp. 99-102.

    Assessment report: Kandhi Tract of Jammu Tehsil, S. 1981, p. 21, and Kotli Tehsil, 1904, pp. 16-19, and Sarna Tehsil, 1914, p. 27, and Ranbir Singh Pur a Tehsil, 1916, p. 19.
48. Assessment Reports: Reasi Tehsil, 1908, pp. 8-43., and Ramnagar Tehsil, 1912, pp. 12-13, and Census 1911, K. Part I, pp. 201 - 208, and I.G.I, 1909, pp. 33-34.
49. S.C. Sharma, "Maharaja Hari Singh-Pioner of Adult Education in Jammu and Kashmir"in Journalism of Social Sciences. Vol. XIV, University of Jammu, 1997, pp. 103-104.
50. Sharp, H., A Note on Education in State of Jammu and Kashmir Calcutta, 1916, p. 2. (Jammu Archive Library). &Sharp, H., op. cit.,p. 2.
51. Census 1921, K. Part I, p. 120. & Census 1931, J&K, Part I, p. 269.
52. Administration report second half of S. 1998 and S. 1999 (194-43 A.D.) p. 13, and A Hand Book of Jammu and Kashmir State, G. J & K, Pol. Dept, 1945, p. 12.
53. Seru, S.L., History and Growth of education in Jammu and Kashmir, 1872-1973 A.D. pp. 110-135.

54. I.G.I., 1909, p. 71 and Adm. Report, p. W.D., J&K, S. 1960 (1903-04 A.D.), p. 3 and Adm. Report, Udhampur Tehsil, 1911, p. 5.
55. G.O.I, F.D., Progs, March 1912, Nos. 10-II/Int I-A, p. 9. & G. J&K, O.E.R. File No. 654/RR.B-20 of 1920, p. 1, and Census 1931, J & K, Part I, p. 14.
56. G. J&K, O.E.R. File. No. 134/R of 1921, p. 21, and I.G.I., 1909, p. 71.

Chapter - 1

Political Awakening in Jammu Region From 1904 - 1953

By political awakening one means a community's awareness of their collective interests and rights. It is acquired through a variety of ways, like the spread of education, newspapers, contacts with outsiders and the outside world, and above all by the feeling that they are being exploited and denied their right by the privileged and the powerful.

Jammu and Kashmir, one of the five hundred and sixty two princely states of India, was carved out by the British, when they broke up the Sikh empire of Maharaja Ranjit Singh and transferred the territories of the Sikh State including Kashmir, Hazara, Jammu and the frontier of Ladakh to Raja Gulab Singh who held Jammu in brief from the Sikhs. The Jammu and Kashmir State, was constituted of three separate linguistic geographic and cultural regions, Kashmir Province, predominately Muslim, Jammu, a part of the foot hills of the Punjab and Ladakh, geographically a part of the Tibetan tableland and inhabited by Buddhists who followed the Tibetan Monastic order. Like the other princely states of India, Jammu and Kashmir was an integral part of the British colonial organisation and was governed by the imperatives of the British paramountcy, not in many ways different from the other princely states of India.The

State administration was organised by the British on the pattern they had adopted in the other princely states and virtually controlled the Government and administration of the State, providing enough of the state revenues to meet the princely extravagance of the ruler and his family. By the end of the 19th century, the state was brought under the administration of the British Government in India and the Maharaja was virtually set aside.[1]

The two parts of the British empire in India, the Britsh India and the India of the Princes, were brought under one authority by the British and perhaps, before their advent, unity of India was not visualized in terms of a political identity, for the Mughal empire, the Sikh empire, the Rajput potentates and the rulers of the central and south Indian states were states apart, which were politically independent of each other and committed to imperatives of political authority representing divergent values and belief systems.[2]

English education exposed the Indian people to liberal reformism of the Nineteenth century which constituted the ideological basis of the British imperialism. The Indian political authority, as it evolved, reflected the essential values of the British liberalist tradition.The rise of the national awakening in India, which formed the basis of the political awakening of the Indian people, grew out of sense of nationalism and the commitment to liberalise reform, which the British liberalism engendered in India. India renaissance awakened the Indian mind to a new freedom and a sense of national identity which represented its being, the social culture and the history of the Indian people.[3]

The Indian renaissance evoked widespread response in the Indian states, including the Jammu and Kashmir State. In Jammu region the political awakening started from 1904 when the **Dogra committee** was constituted which was later named the **Dogra Sadar Sabha**. The Dogra Sadar Sabha committed itself to social and economic reform to elevate the people of the State.[4] Western education too was introduced here only by the end of the 19th century and the first college was established at Jammu in 1907.[5] Here the first newspaper made its appearance much later. Certain administrative measures were initiated to modernise the living condition of the people, like the constitution of the Jammu Municipality. But, on the whole, life moved in old channels in the old way, for the vast majority of the people of Jammu Region. Since the ruling family and most senior officials came from Jammu, which was the seat of power, the average Jammuite had no visible reason to feel exploited. Their ethno-culture links with the rulers made them ignore and to accept the exploitation that the Kashmiri Muslims were later to resent, because of the ethno-cultural divide that made them feel different and discriminated against. The Muslims of Jammu region, mostly Gujjars and Bakerwals had their obvious sense of separate identity and interest, as different from urban Jammu Hindus. But till very recent days they were too backward educationally and economically to be heard or taken notice of. So, for all practical purposes in the period between 1904 and 1953, political awakening worth a study remained confined essentially to the upper caste urban non-Muslims in the three districts where they formed a majority.[6]

However, even in the placid life of Jammu some stirrings were caused by the First World War and the Bolshevik Revolution. People freely talked of the war and large number of Dogra soldiers went out, even abroad to return home as literate and changed persons. The Russian revolution inspired new hopes in the hearts of many who yearned for a more just world and demanded more rights and responsibilties. In the changed condition the first newspaper of Jammu the Ranbir, made its appearance in 1924.[7] The elite of Jammu represented by the Dogra Sabha, began clamouring for the protection of their interests and ambition, and petitioned the Maharaja to debar all outsiders from owing property in this state and taking up government jobs, so that their privileged position remained unchallenged.

In response to their demand the **State Subject Law** was passed by the Maharaja in 1927.[7]

The educationally backward Kashmiri Muslims, however, stood not to gain from this law and resented their virtual second class position in the twin fields of education and jobs. They resented what appeared to them as the discriminatory policy of the Dogra rulers of Jammu and began agitating for reforms on democratic lines. It was essentially in response to their agitation, leading to bloody showdown of 13 July, 1931.[8] It led to the formation of the Muslim conference and then **the Glancy Commission** was appointed and in **1934 the Praja Sabha** was constituted to aid and to advise the ruler.[9]

Unlike the Kahmiri Muslims the Jammuites did not view the Praja Sabha as a weapon to wrest power and right from the absolute ruler. They had every reason to be loyalists and viewed with unease the growing Muslim demand for democratic right and for representation everywhere in proportion to their actual number.[10] However, after the major segment of the Muslim Conference changed themselves into the **National Conference in 1939**, many in Jammu joined it out of an idealistic preference for the individual's rights and justice. But the N.C could never become a major political force among the Hindus of Jammu, while Muslims here were then too backward for effective political mobilization.[11]

The second World War and the August rebellion did stir the people of Jammu. Many went out to fight in Burma and S.E. Asia and returned with their eyes and ears open to the world around them. The threat to India posed by the advancing Japanese army and the Quit India Movement that swept British India did not leave the people of Jammu region untouched.

Their most visible response was the Roti agitation of 1943 against the scarcity that the war, the Bengal famine and other measures relating to the war had brought about.[12]

However, what agitated the people of Jammu region more was their reaction to the Quit Kashmir Movement in the Valley[13], which was viewed by the people here as an attack on the Dogra ruling house and, therefore, on the Dogra Hindus themselves.[14] Scarcely had the state emerged out of the vortex of this agitation when its was overtaken by the storm that was unleashed by the prospects of immediate independence, lapse of paramountcy, and an unparalleled communal holocaust. Obviously, things were going to change soon and almost completely. Yet, initally, both the Hindus and Muslims of Jammu, represented by the Rajya Hindu Sabha and the Muslim Conference, led by Hamidullah Chowdhary, were in favour of the continuance of the ruling dynasty and the maintenance of internal status-quto of the state with an independent status. It was only when the blood baths of the neighbouring Punjab spilled over into this state and that the Hindus and Muslims of Jammu began urging the Maharaja to accede to India and Pakistan, respectively. But even then there was no singnificant movement here for the state's accession to either.[15]

The situation, however, was suddenly changed beyond all expectations when by the end of October 1947, the Pak raiders overwhelmed the State force and arrived within a striking distance of Srinagar. A panic-stricken Maharaja had no option but to seek Indian help by acceding to her, which he did on 27.10.1947. But the accession also meant the institution of popular government. Effective power was soon transferred to the N.C. representing the Kashmir Muslim elite, and the centre of political gravity of this state shifted for ever from Jammu to Srinagar, from upper caste Hindus to the Sunni Muslims of Kashmir.[16] For the elite of Jammu it was too severe a loss of power and status to bear with equanimity, especially when it was the Hindu-Sikh soldiers who had saved the valley.

Moreover, the privileged Hindus resented the Landed Estates Act whereby all large agricultural estates, mostly owned by Rajputs and Kashmiri Pandits, were confiscated without compensation, while the orchards mostly owned by Kashmiri Muslims, were exempted from the purview of this act. The accumulated resentment of the elite of Jammu found its expression in the Praja Parishad agitation organized by Dina Nath Verma and Prem Nath Dogra, with active support of the RSS, the Hindu Mahasabha, the Ram Rajya Parishad and later the Jana Sangh. However, the agitation too dependent on zamindars and sahukars and lacking in support from New Delhi fizzled out after a few years.[17] However, the leaders of this movement and the Jammu non-Muslim, in general, had the vicarious satisfaction of seeing their arch apponent Sheikh Abdullah bundled out of office into prison. His successors, especially Bakshi Ghulam Mohammad, kept the people of Jammu in humour with pro-India rhetoric and by doling out massive aid to ensure the material satisfaction of the people. Jammuites by and large, forgot what they were missing in the mist of what they were receiving.[18]

Even after the partial application of the constitution of India to the State in 1954, the dominance of the Muslims of Kashmir on the government and politics of the state did not end and the movement of the people of Jammu widened its appeal as well as its base. The political awakening of the people in Jammu, formed expression in the manifest political movements: (a) movement for the integration of the state into the Indian constitutional organization (b) Movement for the separation of Jammu and its reorganization into a separate state (c) Regional autonomy for Jammu, institutionalized in political instrumentalities, which represented the people of Jammu.[19]

References

1. Bhat, Koul, Ram Krishan - Page 3-6.
2. Govt. J & K, Political Department File No. 417/5-23 of 1931.
3. Koul Santosh, pp. 25-30.

4. Govt.J&K records Old English, File No. 312/7-C of 1919 and Sarf M.R. Jeevan Chariter, Sher-e-Dugr, Lala Hans Raj (1866-1944) Jammu (1967) pp. 258.
5. Census 1941, J&K Part I & II, pp. 264-280.
6. Puri, Balraj pp. 5-22.
7. A pamphlet from Dogra Sadar Sabha Jammu Plea for State Subject definition and genesis, pp. 1-14.
8. H.H.Govt. J&K Gen. Pol. Dept. file No.485/of 1931 & File No. 13/14 of 1931.
9. Khan, G.H. pp. 18-25.
10. Govt. of J&K File No. 841 of 1931 and File No.424 of 1931.
11. Saraf, M.R. op. cit., pp. 154-156.
12. Sarf, M.R. op. cit., pp. 139-145.
13. Fazili, Manzoor. Socialist Ideas and Movements in Kashmir, 1982. pp. 96-98.
14. File No.424 of 1932.
15. Madhok, Balraj, op. cit. pp. 72- 75.
16. Puri, Balraj, op. cit. pp. 18-23.
17. Edison, David, Sher-e-Kashmir - A lion of Kashmir Sheikh Abdullah, p. 74.
18. Balraj Puri. pp. 34-37.
19. Edison, David, Sher-e-Kashmir, pp. 74-75.

Chapter - 2

The Press: Socio-political Awakening in Jammu Region from 1904-1947

"Swaraj is to a nation what the soul is to the body, and that it is indispensable in order to keep a people alive", observed Aurobindo Ghosh. He further added, "it is not to - be obtained from others by begging but people can get it through this own effort alone". India attained this cherished goal shattering the shackles of slavery on 15th August, 1947.[1]

This spectacular climax was rendered possible by the pioneering efforts made by public men during the half century following the movement of 1857. However country wide awakening was germinated by the intelligentsia or the educated elite, which was largely brought up under the influence of the western culture in its train. Almost unconsciously, as it were, the Indians educated in the west developed the art of expressing this discontent while paying lip service to the British rule. As years rolled by expression of discontent began to get the better of the expression of their loyalty, and consequently in their war of wits, the press had a major role to perform.

Beside the manifestation and causation of political consciousness, among the Indian people, the later part of the 19th century witnessed the following of a variety of socio-religious and cultural movements. Here the press played a seminal role. The significance of the press grow by and large and political leaders, and people engaged in socio-cultural activities, utilized journals and daily news papers for the purpose of disseminating their ideas and ideologies. They were radical in respect of social awakening, and were convinced that without social reforms the political emancipation could not be achieved. Thus the press assumed an important place in the life of the nation and nationalist as well social reforms utilized it as a powerful and effective weapon against the out dated and unhealthy social customs, conventions and the unpopular policies of the government. Thus press crystallized their urge and placed it in the open.[2]

The growth of Socio-political consciousness was not the result of a few agitators but due to the revival of historical traditions and popular will of liberation several factors contributed towards its growth where the unification of India, the wars of Independence which was fought on foreign soil, unification of Italy and Germany, French and Russian revolution, improvements in the means of transport and communication, economic exploitation of India by British, English Education and revival of India's past glories. Besides these factors press also played an important role and became a powerful instrument for mobilizing the people.[3]

The freedom of press in our state is a recent growth. Before 1924, there was not a single newspaper printed or published.[4] Only Jammu and Kashmir Govt. Gazette was the official weekly with a circulätioñ of 900.[5] During 20th Century a great awakening and momentous changes were taking place all over the world and people of the state could not remain unaffected by them. In view of the rapidly changing condition the Jammu and Kashmir govt. was obliged to relax to some extent the iron grip of its press law. As a result some facilities were given for the publication of news papers.[6]

The news papers which limited numbers of people read came from the neighbouring province of the Punjab.**The Civil and Military Gazette, the Tribune of Lahore and a various number of Urdu weekly magazines** were circulated in the State. Whenever any person of Jammu and Kashmir sate intended to write, he had to approach these newspapers and "it all depends on their good will to publish or reject a contribution. The people had 'thus no paper of their own where in they could ventilate their feelings regarding various social and political problems".[7]

It also had seen that the papers which were published form the Punjab and Lahore aroused the communal feelings among the Hindus and Muslims of the Jammu and Kashmir State. Mostly it greatly affected the educated community of the Stäte.[8]

Being a Muslim majority State ruled over by the Hindu king became à matter of concern to both the Hindu and Muslim journalists. They played a significant role in shaping the public opinion along communal lines. The important among the communal news papers were **Akhbiir-I-Am, Lahore, Singh Sahai, Amritsar, Punjab Samachar, Láhore, Aina-I-Kaisar of Jalandhar, Rafiq-I-Hind of Lahore, Punjab Gazette of Rawal Pindi.**[9]

So for as the Jammu region is concerned, it was Lala-Hans Raj, who for the first time spoke for the liberty of speech in 1904 through Dogra Sabha, the first social organization in Jammu. At an annual session of Dogra Sabha in March 1905, Lala Hans Raj moved a resolution demanding liberty of speech, platform in the State. Sardar Bahadur Kajoor Singh while presiding made a forceful speech by saying that this is the birth right of every human being which has been denied to them.[10]

In 1905, Lala Hans Raj started his first paper known as Dogra Gazette in 1906.[11] A letter was written by Anant Ram to Governor of Jammu for permission to publishing a monthly periodical, but no permission was given by the Maharaja.[12] While refusing his permission, a judicial minister remarked, "it was difficult to disconnect politics from questions which had a bearing on the social, moral and educational condition of community". The newspaper he said, "interfere with the politics of the state".[13] In 1906, the Maharaja of Jammu and Kashmir State banned the publication of newspapers. Without his prior permission magazines and newspapers which carried what the government considered violent and offensive articles and attempts of worst type of stirrup hated, were not allowed inside the state.[14]

In 1907 Lala Hans-Raj started another paper known as **Mahajan Nite**.[15] In 1909 His Highness prohibited the news papers related to the discussion on religious, political and cultural matters.[16] In 1910, again a ban was imposed on all the news papers containing reditious ideas and any one found reading or in possession of the disallowed newspapers and pamphlets was punished.[17] Ban was placed on the newspapers were **Rivasat, Sivasat** and **Inqulab** because these newspapers attacked the administration of Dogras and criticised them.[18]

The first newspaper published in 1924 in Jammu was **the Ranbir** by **Mulk Raj Saraf**. He was known as the pioneer of journalism in J & K State. For this publication he had done a lot of hard work. He sent three applications to the Maharaja in which he stated that, "In the period of current reforms such a paper should be started which could be a great instrument for the betterment of the people of state". A sort of campaign was again launched in the national press protesting against the anti- press policy of Darbar. **The Dogra Sahha** then the solitary political organization in the state also stressed the need for starting a newspaper for the state. After a long struggle. the Jammuites got permission for the printing press to start the newspapers in 28th March 1924 and then the first newspaper **Ranbir** was publishtd.[19]

It was welcomed by all people in the state. It was published in Urdu and provided fresh and truth worthy news from all parts of the State. After **Ranbir,** a number of news papers were published i.e. **Chand**, **Amar**, **Mashir, Insaf** & **Waten** from Jammu.

Such was published by Raja Akbar Khan and **Kashmir Sasar** by Balrajpuri.[20]

In 1931 Glancy commission in their recommendation also stressed the freedom of press in the State.[21]

Among the English Newspapers or weeklies mention may be made of the **Kashmir Times** in 1934. It was started weekly and held independent views. It carried some material of education value which made it respect and popular among educated people. The govt. attitude towards it was favourable and it was allowed to be circulated through the schools of the State. Even Maharaja Hari Singh consulted the Kashmir Times in order to put the trends of public opinion. Kashmir Times always stood for the progress of the state in all spheres and never preached communalism or adopted offensive or provocative attitude. Kashmir Times fought against illiteracy and advocated the establishnnt of a net work of primary schools through out state. Reformist and libeial. minded Hindus generally found in this newspaper a valuable ally because of its strong support in favour of social reforms. It also agitated for the protection of the-rights of the State-Subjects It was critical of the govt. policy of giving high-posts to non-state subjects.[22]

All social and political awakening could be attributed, to a great extent to the spread of new ideas by the press. All these news papers infused new blood, new spirit, new life in the mind of the people of Jammu. These papers voiced the grievances of the people and gave expression of their social, economic and political demands. They made people aware of the happening in India and different parts of the country as well as the world.

From the above it is clear that the press in jammu made big advance from 1924-1947. To a great extent the press did echo the social and political awakening in Jammu region. Thus the significance of the period form 1904-1947, was the rise of the press in Jammu region which became powerful medium for creating social-political consciousness.[23]

Indian political consciousness was an over growth of the Indian renaissance. The people in Jammu and Kashmir State were deeply influenced by the Indian renaissance. In fact the struggle for emancipation from foreign rule of the British and the autocracy in the Indian States was a continuity of the Indian renaissance. The press in India reflected the impact of the Indian liberation struggle on the mind of the Indian people.

In that respect the growth of the press in Jammu Region was also the part of Indian Renaissance. The orientation of the people in Jammu to political and social change followed the propagation by press in the Punjab and later in J& K. of the tennents of the Indian liberation struggle. Inside the state Ranhir and other periodicals, journals combined the principlcs of social change and religious reforms with political change and political reforms. From these beginning evolved the movements of self govt. and self rule in the State which was propagated by the press till the liberation of India in 1947.

References

1. Sharma. S.R, The Press - Socio-Political Awakening, New Delhi, 1966, p. 1. 2-. Ahluwalia, M.M.: Freedom struggle 'in India, 1858-1909, Delhi, 1965, p. 5.'
3. Srinivasan, C.R., The Press and the Public, p. 51.
4. Govt. 3. & K, General, Political Deptt. File No. 27/43-C, year 1917, p. 4.
5. Khan, Mohammed Ishaq, History of Srinagar. 1846-1947, Srinagar, p. 175.
6. Govt. J&K, General, Political Dept. File No.27/43-C and 25/ 45-C, year 1917, p. 14.

7. Khan Mohammed lshaq, op. cit., p. 176.
8. Singh, N.K., inter-Communal Relatiors in Jammu and Kashniir, Jammu, p. 84.
9. Khan. G.H, Freedom Movement in Kashm r. 1931-1940. New Delhi. 1980. p. 19.
10. Govt. J&K. (3en. Pot. Dept. File No.51/1-21 of 1906. p. 10.
11. Govt. JK; Gen. Pol. Dept. File No.418/Ps/49 of 1913, p. 11.
12. Govt. J&K. Gen. Pot. Dept. File No. 30 of 1906, p. 6.
13. National Archives of India. Home Dept. Pot. Branch-B. May 1910. No. 148. p. 9.
14. Govt. J&K. Gen. Pot. Dept. File No.334 of 1925. p. 3.
15. Govt. J&K. Gen. Pot. Dept. File No 418/PS/49 of 1913. p. 5.
16. Govt. J&K. Gen. Pol. Dept. File No.27/43-C year 1917, p. 7.
17. National Archives of India. Home Dept., Pot. May 1910, No. 44. p. 22.
18. Govt. J&K. Gen. Pot. Dept. File No. 39/3 of t919. p. 7.
19. Saraf. M.R.. Fifly Years in Journalism. p. 24.
20. Yassien. Mohammad: Freedom Siniggle in Kashmir-; p. 184.
21. Khan. G.H.. op. cit.. p. 30.
22. Khan. Mohammed Ishaq. op. cit. p. 186. the Indian people.
23. Political Awakening in Jammu Region From 1904-1 95.

Chapter - 3

The Dogra Sadar Sabha: A Social and Political Organization of Jammu Province from 1904 to 1957

Certain social organizations existed even in traditional India for regulating the affairs of different caste and economic groups. But in this modern sense these came into being only in the later 19th century, when different elite groups realized the advantage of forming caste organizations to press for facilities for their fellow members, to settle disputes amicably and to eradicate social evils.

The last decade of 19th century, in J & K State, gave birth to socio-religious reform movements which brought an awakening among the people[1] and had an important impact not only in social outlook of the people but had also tremendous political consequences. These movements roused the people to a sense of self-reassertion for the status of equality in the society, economy and political spheres of the political systems.[2] It was only because of, when the people have a sense of security of life and prosperity, with introduction of western education, construction of Jammu-Sialkot Railway link in 1890, and the exchange of ideas among the people.[3]

It was evident from the fact that there was a complete ban on the formation of all types of socio and religious societies in the 19th century. The previous sanction of the Govt. was essential for the formation of the society.[4] Towards the close of 19th century the ban was removed and a number of social organizations emerged for protecting the interest of particular society and reforming social evils. One among them was Dogra Sadar Sabha.[5]

Whenever we talk about the political and social awakening in Jammu province, we talk about the Dogra Sadar Sabha, the oldest political and social organization, when two great Dogra visionaries, *Lala Hans Raj Mahajan* and his associate, *Sahib Zada Hazarat Shah* laid the foundation of *Dogra Committee,* which later changed its name *Dogra Sadar Sabha Jammu in* 1904.[6]

To discuss the various problems and difficulties of the people of the community, a meeting of about seven hundred citizens belonging to different caste and religion was convened at Jammu on 12th June I904.[7] Here a unanimous resolution was adopted to form a Dogra Sadar Sabha, to promote the cause of the people of Jammu and to realize its cherished desires and aspirations.[8]

In earlier stages the Sabha was dubbed as a "loyalist" body established, to support the Dogra Raj. Those holding this view said that Dogra Sadar Sabha had been established with the blessings of Maharaja Pratap Singh and his brother Raja Amar Singh. The huge register entirely written in Urdu in the hands of Lala Hans Raj contains the text of all the resolution passed by the Sabha in its earlier stage. No separate order permitting the formation of the Sabha appears to have issued. The Maharaja's approval of the resolution register itself was considered to be more important as it meant his direct involvement in the Sabha. For establishing its branches, however, the Sabha applied for permission and it was granted formal permission.[9] This indicates the support of the royal household in the formation of the first social organization in the state, which includes all men irrespective of any distinction of caste or religion.[10]

The first dignitaries of this organization were elected as under[11]:

1.	Pandit Ganesh Dass Shastri	President
2.	Mian Jawala Singh	Vice President
3.	Sheikh Ali Mohammad	Vice President
4.	Lala Hans Raj Mahajan	Secretary
5.	Pandit Manohar Nath Koul	Assistant Secretary
6.	Sahib Zada Hazrit Shah	Assistant Secretary
7.	Lala Jaipal	Treasurer

Aims and Objectives: At its first meeting the Committee outlined its aims and objectives:

1. Strengthening social, cultural unity by promoting mutual cooperation and good will among different social and cultural groups in the state.
2. Peaceful persuasion of the Government to accede to the genuine demands of the people.
3. Struggle for social, cultural and economic developments of the state.
4. Rousing social and political consciousness among the people.
5. Bringing into the notice of the authorities the wrong actions and the politics of the government.
6. Pressurizing the State Government for the spread of education.
7. Struggling for granting more and more rights to the permanent resident of the state.[12]

Activities of the Sabha

Previously, there was a ban on the Press and the platform in J & K State but with the strong determination of Lala Hans Raj Mahajan, succeeded in getting the permission to start the newspaper, Dogra Gazette in 1905, soon after the formation of the Sabha.[13] To give wide publicity to its programmes and policies and to bring into notice of the

Government the demands of the people, the Dogra Sadar Sabha started publications through periodicals and Dogra Gazette in 1907. Since almost all the resolutions passed by the Dogra Sadar Sabha were published in it. These periodicals had considerable effect in pressing for redress of the grievances of the people. It also awakened social and political consciousness among the people of this region.[14]

Lala Hans Raj, the real founder of this Sabha and the greatest social reformer of this region in the 20th century, worked selflessly with great enthusiasm and undaunted courage for its progress. By 1920, he had succeeded in establishing its branches in each district of the province i.e., Kathua, Udhampur and Reasi, etc.[15] The Sabha extended its branches outside the state. During the thirties one such branch was established at Karachi to help the people of this state seeking employment there.[16]

The Dogra Sadar Sabha made earnest efforts to eradicate mass illiteracy among the people. Though the Sabha opened no educational institution, it urged the government, through resolutions passed from time to time, to impart free and compulsory primary education and to open colleges, high schools and technical institutions.[17] It also voiced the need of imparting educations to Harijans and of granting liberal scholarships to students. These resolutions did not carry weight with the government; because the number of Sabhaites was usually quite influential people.[18] Beside this, the Sabha also granted financial assistance to needy students out of its own funds.[19]

The major problem to which the Sabha devoted its attention was the protection to the rights of state subjects in the services. Since the very existence, the Dogra Sadar Sabha was seized with the fact that many outsiders were employed in government jobs in the state. Besides, trade and industry also were mainly in their hands. This was the first organization in the state to demand preference for state subjects over outsiders in government services, trade and industry.[20]

The Voice of the Dogra Sabha was so strong that the government at least passed a law regarding 'state subjects', in April, 1927. Even after the enforcement of the term 'state subject' the Sabba continued bringing into the notice of the government cases of fictitious state subject certificates issued to outsiders and succeeded in getting many of these bogus certificates cancelled.[21]

Dogra Sadar Sabha defined in their pamphlets "A plea for state subject definition and genesis" that the direct outcome of the short sighted selfish policy of the outsiders who taking unfair advantage of this position in the administration of the state brought the things to such a point that necessity was felt for a protection measure being adopted.[22]

The rights of state subjects in services were finally secured and purchase of immoveable property by non-state subjects was banned. This law with minor amendments is in force even to this day.[23]

Political Role

Besides its social activities, The Dogra Sadar Sabha taking part in political affairs also during the reign of Maharaja Hari Singh. It favoured the activities of Indian National Congress in Freedom Movement.[24] Lala Hans Raj Mahajan who had earned the title of **Sher-I Duggar** and **the old Dogra General** went a step further and wrote to the General Secretary of all India Congress in 1929 that the Dogra Sabha was virtually the Congress in Jammu and was following an identical programme and should be allowed to send delegates to attend the Congress Session being held in Lahore.[25] So in 1929 some members of the Dogra Sabha were present and they declared the Sabha to be "The Congress Committee of Jammu and Kashmir State".[26] On this the British Minister in Maharaja Hari Singh's council,

Mr. G.E.C. Wakefield described it as an act of treason on the part of Mr. Màhajan who wanted to join his hands with the enemies of the British.[27]

Besides this Dogra Sadar Sabha was in the favour of Swadeshi movement and propagated the use of Khaddar. They waged a fight to boycott the use of foreign goods.[28] In 1930 when Gandhi ji gave a call against foreign goods; it was Dogra Sabha, which organized a *'Holi'* of foreign clothes.[29] Lala Hans Raj and Sri Nivas Shah Magotra collected foreign clothes and burnt them in Purani Mandi and in front of city Thana at Jammu.[30]

For taking active part in politics and interfering in the state administration, Maharaja Hari Singh on the advice of Mr. G.E.C. Wakefield declared the Dogra Sadar Sabha as 'unlawful body' by his order dated 9th may 1930.[31]

On the birthday ceremony of Maharaja Han Singh, in Oct. 1931, a proclamation was read in which a ban was removed on the Dogra Sabha.[32]

In the early thirties The Dogra Sadar Sabha raised a strong voice for the establishment of a popular assembly in the state.[33] The state government acceded to the growing demand of the people and an assembly, called Praja Sabha, was constituted in 1934.[34] Lala Hans Raj, one of the most prominent members of the Dogra Sadar Sabha, was also elected unopposed to Praja Sabha, on 9th July 1936.[35] Being a fearless and selfless person, Lala Hans Raj always favoured such policies of the government that were in the welfare of the people and criticized those that were not in their interest. Besides other things, he always pleaded for the establishment of local bodies, greater civic rights for the people, development of cottage industry, uplift of Harijans, welfare of the peasantry and labourers and increased job opportunities for educated youths of the state.[36]

After 1947, The Dogra Sadar Sabha became, more or less, a political organization taking a more active part in the political affairs of the state. Since 1953 it participated actively in the deliberation of the National Conference.[37] On 6th May 1957, The Dogra Sadar Sabha adopted a resolution to work for the victory of the National Conference in the election to the state assembly.[38] For extending this co-operation the National Conference allowed two members of the Dogra Sadar Sabha, Wazir GangaNath and Thakur Rattan Singh Jamwal to contest the election for Legislative Council on party tickets and they went in it.[39]

To conclude we can say that Dogra Sadar Sabha was a socio-Political organization which not only worked for the people of Jammu province, but for the whole state and introduced a number of reforms for the welfare of the state.

References

1. Census 1911, K, Part I, pp. 211, 212.
2. Yassien, Mohammad, History of Freedom Struggle in Jammu and Kashmir, 1980, p. 89.
3. Kapoor, M.L., Social, Economic History of J& K State (1885-1 925), Jammu, p. 193.
4. Govt. J & K., Old English records, File No. 242\P-38 of 1912; J & K Govt. Old English Records, File No. 34/19 12, p. 4; and Census of India, 1931, Vol. XXII, Part I, p. 141.
5. J & K Govt., Old English Records, File No. 242/P-38 of 1912, p. 7; and Kumar, Sudarshan, "Social History of Jammu City from 1885-1947", Unpublished Thesis, p. 105.
6. Sharma, B. P., Kashmir Times, Sunday, 15 Oct., 1989; 'Role of Dogra Sadar Sabha',p. 5.-
7. Govt. J & K. Old English Records, F. No. 312/7-c of 1919, p. 3; and Saraf, Mulk Raj, Jeewan Cnaritar, Sher-I-Duggar Lala Hans Raf Mahajan (1800-1 944), (Urdu), Jammu, 1967, p. 256.
8. Govt. J & K, O.E.R F. No. 312/7-c of 1919, pp 3; Govt. J & K, G.E.R., F. No. 1621 of 1922, p. 7.
9. Sharma, B.P., op. cit.
10. Govt. J & K, Old English Records, F. No. 312/7-c of 1919, pp. 3-5; Govt. J&K, General English Records, F. No. 1621 of 1922, p. 7.

11. Saraf, Mulk Raj, Riyasat Jammu wa Kashmir Kay Pratham Lokpriya Naita, Sher-I-Duggar Lala Hans Raj, 1866-1944, Jammu, 1968, pp. 15-16.
12. The Dogra Gazette, Weekly (Urdu) Jammu, 5, 1935, p. 2. Ram Wazir Ganga, President Dogra Sadar Sabha, Dogron Ki Haqiqi Tarzman Dogra Sabha (Urdu). Jammu, 1959, p. 2.
13. Govt. J & K General records Political Dept. FileNo. 51/1-71 of 1906 and Sharma, B.P., op. cit.
14. *Ibid.*
15. Govt. J & K, Old Eng. Record., F. No. 265/129/Misc. of 1920, p. 1.
16. The Dogra Gazette, Dec. 17, 1935, p. 11.
17. Resolution Passed by the Dogra Sadar Sabha in the Dogra Gazette, Dec. 5, 1935, p. 2; Govt. J & K general Records, Pol. Dept. F. No. 229, year 1920.
18. Govt. J & K, O.E.R, F. No. 231P-47 of 1912, p. 1; and Govt. J & K, O.E.R, F. No.264/23-c of 1917, pp. 56 to 58.
19. Gupta, Kishori Lal, "Social History of Jammu Province from 1901-1981", unpublished Thesis, p. 108.
20. Govt. J & K, General English Records., F. No. 97/63-g of 1924, pp. 5 to 23; Govt. J & K, O.E.R., File No.264/23-c of 1917, pp. 1-15.
21. The Dogra Gazette, Sep. 26 ,1935, p. 7; Oct. 3, 1935, pp. 8-10; Oct. 17, 1935, p. 8; Dec. 5, 1935, p. 2.
22. A Pamphlet from Dogra Sadar Sabha, Jammu, Plea for State Subject: Definition and Genesis, pp. 1-14.
23. Sharma, B.P., op. cit., p. 8.
24. Order of Maharaja Hans Singh, dated 9 May, 1930, G.O.R, F. No. 326, p. 6 of 1930; Crown File. No. 291, File No. 22-P of 1930, p. 8.
25. A pamphlet from Dogra Sadar Sabha Jammu, Plea for State Subject: Definition and Genesis, pp. 1-14.
26. Order of Maharaja Hari Singh, dated 9 may, 1930, G.O.R, F. No. 326 of 1930 pp. 6, 22-29.
27. A Pamphlet from Dogra Sadar Sabha, Jammu, Plea for State Subject: Definition and Genesis, pp. 1-14.
28. Govt. J & K General Records, Pol. Dept. File. No. 93/63-g of 1924; Govt. J&K G.R.P. Dept. File. No. 264/23 of 1917.

29. Khan, G.H., Freedom Movement in Kashmir 1931-40, Jammu, 1980, pp. 52,54.
30. Some written letters available in the Dogra Sadar Sabha, Jammu.
31. Order of Maharaja Hari Singh, dated 9 May, 1930, G.O.R., F. No. 326-P of 1930, p. 6; Crown File No. 291. p. 8.
32. Govt. J & K General Records, Pol. Dept. File No. 327/-Year 1931.
33. The Dogra Gazette, 5 Dec., 1935, p. 2.
34. Saraf, Mulk Raj, Jammu and Kashmir Encyclopaedia, 1846 to 1946, p. 2.
35. Saraf, Mulk Raj, Jeewan Chanter, Sher-I-Duggar Lala Hans Raj Mahajan (1866-1944) (Urdu), 1967, pp. 101 to 104.
36. *Ibid.*
37. Ram,Wazir Ganga, op. cit., pp. 6-11.
38. *Ibid.,* p. 11.
39. *Ibid.,* pp. 12-13.

Chapter - 4

Socio Religious Reform Movements - (Arya Samaj in Jammu region from 1890 - 1947)

We cannot deny that Arya Samaj had became a potent voice in India's Socio-Religious and political re-generation. A few scholars have attempted to prepare a comprehensive work on Socio religious and political aspects[1] of the Arya Samaj movement in Jammu and Kashmir state and failed in their mission to throw ample light on the social and religious movements in Jammu region.

Aims and Objective of Arya Samaj in Jammu Rigion

1. Activities of Arya Samaj in different Districts of Jammu region.
2. To spread vadic principles.
3. To remove untouchability.
4. Their work for Dooms and Meghas
5. Reaction of Muslims and non -Muslims.
6. Maharaja's reaction.
7. Shuddi movements (Purification).
8. Their political role.
9. Emergence of consciousness through social reforms.

The Socio-religious reform movements were a necessary prelude to the awakening in the country. Certain social organisation existed even in the traditional India for regulating the affairs of different cast and economic groups. But in the Modern sense these came into being only in the later 19th century, when different elite groups realized the advantage of forming caste organisation to press for facilities for their fellow members, to settle dispute amicably and to eradicate Social evils.[2]

The last decade of 19 Century, gave birth to Socio-religious reform movements in Jammu and Kashrnir State. These reform movements brought about a revolution in the thoughts of the people and Society through vedas and Ancient Iiterature. The people of this revolution were influenced by the similar movements in British India whose aim was to up-lift Indian Society form the abyss of superstition obscurantism and stagnation into which it had fallen.[3] These movements in the State represented the nascent urge to change the prevailing social and religious frame in the preparation for a political change. These movements roused[4] the people to a sense of self reassertion for a status of equality in the society, economy and political spheres of political system.[5]

It is evident from the fact that in Jammu and Kashmir, There was a complete ban on the formation of all types of socio-religious societies in the 19th century.[6] But towards the close of 19th century the ban was removed and number of Social- religious organisations emergrd for protecting the interest of particular society and reforming social evils.[7]

The people of J&K were responsible for these reform movements because they want to bring some change in the Society.[8] The leading men from upper and middle classes like their counterparts in the rest of the Sub-continent were "economically prosperous, educationally advanced and socially esteemed". 'The leaders of these movements played a vital role, however in bringing out the peop1e from the rut of ignorance and inferiority complex. They infused in them spirit of self confidence, self dignity and self help. These movements brought in them a sense of civic rights and up held their Ideas mainly on the basis of reason and some of them openly questioned the authority of Ancient scriptures, which the western education had introduced in the Sub-continent.[9]

Among one of these earliest organisation was Arya Samaj which emerged in Jammu and Kashmir state in the last decade of the 19th century.

Arya Samaj in Jammu region

Arya Samaj, being the greatest Socio-religious reform movements in India[10] found its enthusiastic adherents in large number in northern and western parts of India during the last decade of 19th Century. After shifting the head quarters of the Arya to Lahore in 1877, a network of its branches were spread through out the Punjab and the movement gained great momentum.[11]

In Jammu and Kashmir, Arya Samaj was the first organization to start a socio-religious reform movement.[12] Recognised by the state it had established various branches of its office in to two regions i.e. Kashmir and Jammu region.[13]

As for as the Jammu region is concerned, Arya Samaj remained confined for a long time because of its religious reform movements.[14] These movements spread to Jammu region because of its close cultural and commercial contracts with Punjab. The districts of Jammu, Mirpur and Kathua were greatly effected by the activities of the Samaj because of their proximity to Gurdaspur, Sialkot and Jehlum district of the Punjab. Apart from this many Arya Samajist who were employed in the State services did appreciable work to spread this movement in Jammu region.[15]

By the close of 1891, a branch of Arya Samajist had been found at Jammu. It is now called **Arya Samaj Daya Nand**

Marg, Jammu. The credit goes to the Punjabi traders and state officials of Jammu.[16] Another branch of the Arya Samaj, originally called **Nagar Samaj** was established at Jammu, in 1895. Now it is called **Arya Samaj Purani Mandi,** Jammu.[17]

Being based on monotheism infallibility of the vedas and shorn of idolatory, polytheism, Brahamanical domination[18] and the intricacies of a rigid caste system[19], the movement got ready acceptance both among the educated as well as the lower strata of the Society.[20] According to it vedas contained all the knowledge imparted to man by God and essential of modern science could also be trace that. As elsewhere, the ten principles of the Arya Samaj showed positive result in attracting large number of adherents in this region because it was against the cast distinctions and social inequality.

While in the whole of this state there were only 79 Arya Samajis in 1901, This number rose to 1,047 in 19ll and to 23,116 in 1921,[21] of whom 22,994 were in Jammu alone.[22] By the year 1931, the number of Arya Samaj in this region had gone upto 92,725, showing an increase of 303.2 percent since 1921[23]. This startling increase was mainly because of the vigorous propaganda and proselytizing activities among the Harijans by the Arya Samaj.[24]

Apart from Jammu, it also led its effect on the other parts i.e. districts of Kathua and Mirpur by the end of the twenties and also few Tehsil headquarters.[25]

In 1941, the number of adherents of the Arya Samaj in Jammu region was 85,656[26]. The slight fall in 1941 was due to a big conference of the Harijans of this region was convened at Kheri village in Jammu district by Arya Samajist, in which a decision was taken that the Harijans should got themselves recorded as Hindus instead of Arya Samajist, in the census of 1941, This they did because of the growing numerical strength of the Muslims and their religious propaganda.[27]

Role of Arya Samaj

The Arya Samaj was the first organisation to start Socio-religious reform movements among the Hindus in this region. Being a leveling force among the Hindus repudiating and breaking down the barriers of the caste system,laid emphasis on proselytizing activities.[28] With this it infused fresh vitality and a sense of brotherhood among the Hindus.[29]

Social Role

The Arya Samaj introduced reforms of the most revolutionary characters in social field. It condemned a large number ôf old customs, institutions, beliefs and ceremonies. It denounced in strong terms the worship of idols, performance of shradas and distinction of cast by birth. It also denounced child marriage and encouraged widow remarriage.[30]

In Jammu and Kashmir Arya Samaj worked with two fold objectives, to spread vadic principles. Firstly, its activities involved the working of Shuddi (Purification) programme which it had adopted to reclaim those people who at different times left the original vadic religion and had gone over Islam or Christianity. Secondly, its rembers were actively engaged in the Indian freedom struggle.[31]

Taking inspiration from the Punjab and all Indian Shuddi Sabha, the Arya Samaj in Jammu region stated vigorous movement for the reclamation of the depressed classes to the Arya fold, inspite of strong opposition from Orthodox Hindus. In this process the **Arya Samaj Purani Mandi**, Jammu and Arya Samaj **Dayanand Marg**, Jammu took the leading and considerable success.[32]

During the decade of 1911 to 1921, ceaseless propaganda started by zealous workers and succeeded in attracting large number of Meghas and Dooms to this faith in Jammu District, particularly in Ranbir Singh Pura Tehsil.[33] Maharaja Pratap Singh, disapprove the programme of shuddhi, by saying that Dooms and Meghas have never been considered as Hindus and activities of Arya Samaj in converting them into Hinduism was very much to be deprecated as the propaganda against the tenants of Orthodox Hinduism.[34]

The Arya Samaj Dayanand Marg, Jammu carried on its proselytizing activities in Udhampur, Bhaderwah, Kishtwar and Reasi Tehsil also. There too, large number of people belonging to depressed classes availed of the opportunity of Shuddi (Purification).[35] The branch of Arya Samaj at Mirpur also achieved substantial success in this direction. It carried propaganda work in Mirpur, Kotli, Rajouri and Reasi tehsil.[36] The branch of Arya Samaj at Udhampur also did much appreciable work in this direction with the help of Shaddi Sabha of Sialkot.[37]

In Jammu region Arya Samaj worked with much vigor to remove the untouchability through Shuddi[38] Consequently in the mid of 1917, some Orthodox Hindus started anti- Arya Samaj preaching in Jammu and criticised the activities of Arya Samaj. A tense situation emerged between the two sections of Hinduism.[39]

In the year 1917 Muslims also criticized the activities of the Arya' Samaj. Anjuman-i-Isiamia, organised a big gathering[40] of Muslims in which prominent Ulema from India also participated.They also resented the Arya Samaj Suddhi movement.

Educational Role

In the field of Education too the Arya Samaj had made commendable contribution.[41] In order to diffuse knowledge and dispel ignorance, the Arya **Samaj Purani Mandi**, Jammu established **Arya Kanya-Vidyalaya**, Jammu, **D. AV High School**, Jammu, **Arya Kanya Vidyalaya Rehari** Jammu. These institutions are still flourishing. Apart from these, Patshalas were opened by the Arya Samaj at **Narayana, Chhamb, Akhnoor, Barnot** and **Ranbir Singh pura** in Jammu district and in Kathua, Poonch, Mirpur, Nowshera and Udhampur tehsils. By the year 1961, most of had been closed down for one reason or other. However a middle school in Kathua and Karya Vidyalaya at Udhampur still survive.[42]

The holo-caust of 1947 gave a severe blow to the Arya Samaj movements, particularly in Pak-occupied areas of Mirpur, Kotli, Bimber, Rajouri and Poonch. All most the entire population of these areas became refugees.[43] However the restoration of normal conditions and rehabilitation of refugees of these areas, mostly in Jammu and its surroundings, the devoted followers again started their work, and by the year 1961, separate branches of Samaj had been established at Kotli colony, Bakshi Nagar and Gandhi Nagar in Jammu city by its enthusiastic followers. Their number increased in fifties because of literacy, social consciousness and propaganda activities of the Movement.[44]

Political Role

Beside playing important role in Socio-religious field, It also played an important role in the political field in Jammu region and created communal feelings among the masses of Jammu region.[45]

On 12th of May 1907, that Sant Singh of Arya Samaj and a teacher in Jammu High School was dismissed and expelled from the state for publishing a pamphlet "the first step of India towards Independence."[46] It became more active immediately after the Non-Cooperation Movement which was started by Gandhi ji in British India in 1920. The political activities of the Arya Samaj manifested themselves when it called the people to meet in Sammelans, organised public meetings and took out processions. The Samaj became, in some cases "entirely of an extremist political character".[47] It enlisted membership from the non-official clerks and teachers as well as many high officials of the state,[48] and collected subscriptions for the tilk funds. Its annual sessions were marked with the singing praise of India, The Swaraj and the leaders of the Indian freedom struggle. Its leaders in Jammu preached in favour of "Non-cooperation including boycotting schools and renouncing of government files and in some other way exciting remarks had made.[49]

Lecturers on political themes such as "how to attain Swaraj" were delivered to the people. Referring to the Government repressive policies, crubing the political Movement, the leaders would say, "The day is coming when the Whistling of a Railway engine will be considered political.The leaders urged the people to act boldly with out fear and exhibit their courage by courting imprisonment.[50]

Arya Samaj Jammu celebrated its anniversary onthe 21st, 22, 23rd of march 1925. On the 21st, a procession was taken out in the city and on the other days meetings were held in the premises of the local Dogra hall. Pt Vishnu Bandhu, in the course of his speech, remarked that the removal of the cause of untouchability[51] was essential for the attainment of Swaraj.

Arya Samaj remained in the fore front to create National consciousness among the people of Jammu. But it could sacred a foot hold among the liberal and progressive minded Hindus only. As a result when Muslims saw the leading Arya Samajist at the helm of freedom struggle, they kept them self aloof of it. It was one of the causes of the activities that Arya Samaj created division among Hindus and Muslims during National Struggle.[52]

The attitude of State Government authorities towards the Arya Samaj was not sympathetic because it will not a well come movement for the State Government. The Chief minister of the State, under the standing orders from the Maharaja was required to closely watch the activities of the Samaj and take strict action against its activities.[53]

Some time Samaj was not allowed to hold Jalsa (Meetings). As a matter of fact, Pratap Singh adopted hostile attitude towards the Samaj. It was mainly due to this reason that police force was asked to watch secretly and report on the activities of the Samaj. How ever the Arya Samaj inspired by noble ideas and was determined to achieve its ideals. So inspite of the cripping hardship it continued with its mission.[54]

To conclude we can say that Arya Samaj played a very crucial role in promoting an awareness of the problems in Jammu region and a sense of unity among the people. Its efforts to remove the social evils and inequalities in society and condemnation of superstitions and narrowness of outlook also helped people to become aware of their political plight. It also played an important role for rediscovering Indian's past and literature in various Indian languages which revived a pride in India's cultural heritage and its glorious past.

References

1. Kour, Ravinder, Political Awakening in Kashmir, p. 53.
2. Census 1911, K.Part I, pp. 211-212.
3. Khan, G.H., Freedom Struggle in Kashmir.
4. Kour, Ravinder., p. 53.
5. Yassin, Mohammad, Freedom Struggle in Jammu and Kashmir, p. 89.
6. Khan, GM, p. 49.
7. Yassan, Mohammad., pp. 89-90.
8. Bamzai, P.N.K ,Struggle for freedom,7P.724, File no 242/P-38 of 1912,P.7, Govt. J&K Old Eng. Record.
9. File no. 242 of 38 of 1912, PP.7-8 and File no 02/Mis/I 921,p. 2
10. Census 1911, Vol.XV, p. 129.
11. Risley, Sir Herbert, The people of India, London, 1908, p. 243.
12. Yassin, Mohammad, p. 90
13. File no. 215 of 1910, P.7. Govt. J&K Govt. Pol. Record G.P.R.
14. *Ibid.*
15. Vidyarthi Shree Harish Chander, Jammu and Kashmir, Raiya Main Arya Samaj KA Itihas (Hindi), Jammu, 1978, op. It, p. 5.
16. List of societies, sabha and. Anjumans in J&K, File no. 312/2-C/1919. P.18-17, lbid, p. 19.

17. *Ibid,* p. 19.
18. Khan, G.H., P. 49 and Yassin; Mohammad, p. 90.
19. Census 1931, J&K Part I, p. 296.
20. Rai, Lajpat., (edited by (Sri Ram Sharma) A History of Arva Samaj, an account of its origin, doctrines and activities with a biographical sketch of founder, Calcutta) 1967, p. 40.
21. Census 1921, K Part I p. 62.
22. Census 1931, J&K Part I, p. 296.
23. *Ibid.*
24. Census 1931, J&K Part I, p. 321.
25. File no. 162 of 1922, P.P 6 to 10 Govt J&K, Govt. Pol. Records and Census, 1931, J&K Part I p. 32.
26. Census 1941, J&K Part I & II, p. 337.
27. Vidyapeeth, Shri Harish Chander, Op. cit, p. 102.
28. Encyclopaedia of Social Work in India Vol. I, 1968, p. 383.
29. Kambla, J.R., Rise and awakening of depressed classes in India, New Delhi, 1979, p. 38.
30. Gupta 1 Sudarshan Kumar, Social History of Jammu Op. Cit, p. 108.
31. Sing, K.Nirmali t_rn Ajj1tj P.112. year.
32. Census 1921, K. Part I, p. 62.
33. *Ibid.,* pp. 62, 63.
34. *Ibid* and File No. 215 of year 1910 p. 9.
35. Vidyarthi, Shri Harsh Chander, p. 50.
36. Census 1921, K Part.l, p. 62.
37. Vidyarthi, Shri Harsh Chander, p. 50.
38. File no. 215 of 1917, Govt. J&K Phol. Deptt. p. 7.
39. File no. 261/28-C of 1917 p. 5.
40. Saraf Yusaf Mohammad., Op. Cit p. 35.
41. Census 1931 J&K part. l, p. 264.
42. Gupta, Kishori lal., A social history of Jammu province from 1900 to 1961, p. 294.
43. Vidyarthi, Shri Harsh Chander., p. 21.
44. *Ibid.,* pp. 21 to 23.
45. File no.261/28 of 1921, P.20, file no. 32/-C of 1917 and File no. 157/C of 1911, p. 7.

46. G.E.O.R J&K Archive, File no.261/28 of 1921-C and 1917, p. 3 and File no. 157/C of 1911 p. 16.
47. File no.157/-Il of 1921- P.D.G.R, p. 16.
48. Semi-Official letter from Governor of Jammu to Home Minister to His Highness Vide 526-P. Dated April, 1911, Ibid. p. 17-18.
49. File no. 589/CH, Semi Official (Confidential) date 8 April. Ibid p. 19.
50. Report of G.C Rampal, A.S.P Jammu Dated April 8, 1921, Ibid. pp. 16-21.
51. Daily reports, J&K Govt. Archive, 1924-25 p. 17.
52. Khan,G.H. op. Cit,. p. 104.
53. J&K Govt. His. Highness, Personal Records, File no. 71 of 1914, p. 6 File no. 125/46 year 1919, p. 15.
54. Sharma, B.P, Article in Kashmir times, Sunday 15 October. 1989, Role of Dogra Sabha, P.5, File no.125/46 year 1919, p. 16.

Chapter - 5

Tyag Murti—Sardar Budhsingh

The history of Political awakening in Jammu Province will remain incomplete if the role played by some of the elder public men belonging to Jammu Province, remain unwritten and untold.

There were a number of great personalities those who were highly educated and patriotic in the beginning of the 20th Century. A platform for them was thus provided during the regime of Maharaja Pratap Singh. It was then the elements roused their voice for the State Subjects, when there was no liberty of speech or press or of reformation.

Some of the leaders were Lala Hans Raj, Sadar Budh Singh, Ram Chand Duby, General Samunder Khan, Munshi Asadullah Advocate, Shri Chattar Singh and Lala Mullk Raj Saraf.[1]

Among them one shining personality was Sardar Budh Singh, to whom people called **Tyag Murti**. He was the founder of the political agitation in the State. Before, him every politics was related to the Darbar i.e. Anti Government. He was the first mass politician of the State.[2]

He was a Sikh revolutionary of the Jammu province who started his carrier as a camp-clerk in the employment of the State Government. He soon rose to the position of district collector in the State Government. Budh Singh even in his service showed exemplary courage, honesty and uprightness to deal with the people.[3]

From 1915, he started his political activities in Jammu and Kashmir State. When Gandhi ji started the Civil Disobedience Movement, he was the only man to start their agitation with Congress and showed his sympathy towards them.[4]

As a revenue officer he has an opportunity of touring the villages and his contact with the masses convinced him that they were being crushed by an administration which knew no human sympathy.[5] In his tour diaries, he wrote to the supervisor officer the ill committed with the land revenue system, the rigours of Begar, the Rampart administrative corruption, untouchability, social evils, general backwardness and poverty of people.[6]

He wrote a letter to Maharaja Partap Singh in which he said, "your Highness remained busy in Puja and other religious ceremonies while your officers are crushing your subjects under their heavy weight. Corruption is also rampant. The villagers are made to undergo the rigours of Begar, your Highness, subjects are leading a miserable life. Puja alone will not help you to attain salvation unless you take steps to relieve your subjects of their miseries."[7]

In due courage of time the state Government felt concemed about what he did and again chastised him for what he wrote however, Budh Singh struggled alone and undunted. He was the first person who fought for the social, economic and political rights of the people.[8]

He was fearless and courageous. In. 1920 he addressed two public meetings in Hazuri Baghat, Srinagar. There he raised his voice to protest against the forceable labour employed by the Gpvernment agency without payment. This was not the first voice ever raised publicly against the

Maharaja's rule for which Budh Singh was prepared to face the consequences even if he were asked to quit his service.

In his speeches, he charged the State Officials of corruption and harassment of the people of the State. He accused all the High and low officials of bribery and black mail[9] and appealed to Maharaja Pratap Singh to enhance he pay of the State offices so that they would desist from corruption.[10] He advised state servents to live a simple life and he exhorted the people to take Swadeshi and give up using foreign clothes which he marked as the beginning of the freedom struggle. He himself had, however, already taken to the use of Khadar.[11]

In 1922 Budh Singh wrote a letter to Raja Hari Singh and appealed him for speedy reforms in the administrative set up of the State.[12] He laid before the Raja the following suggestions i e.[13]

1. Establishing of Panchayat System
2. Definition of the right of the State Subject
3. Removal of the untouchability
4. Spread of education
5. Freedom of press and Platform.
6. Crubing the corruption
7. Improvement of trade and commerce
8. Maintenance of Justice
9. Responsible Government
10. Representation of Assembly
11. Use of Swadeshi
12. Abolition of Begar
13. Construction of Roads and Bridges

In 1923, he joined the Akali Movement which was started at Srinagar.[14] In 1925 he finally resigned from the post of Deputy Commissioner[15] to devote his life for the Up-liftment of poor, oppressed and down trodden people of rural areas irrespective of their religion, caste or region. The day he resigned, he addressed a large number of gathering of people in Srinagar in which he said that the condition of the Sikhs was extremely deplorable. He assured that he had laid down his office to serve his community and the people of the state in general.[16]

The Sikh and the Dogra people had given him high respecte and thrice he was elected the president of Dogra Sabha and presided over the annual session. He used the Dogra Sabha as a platform for his political purposes and had given the references of freedom movement launched by Gokhlee, Tilak and Gandhi ji in India. He protested against Maharaja on his ban on Dogra Sabha and Ranbir Paper.[17]

The result was that, he was arrested and confind in Bahu fort and two of his book-sets **Kisan-Ki-Dastan** and **Giribon-Ke-Dukh-RAJ** confiscated.[18]

In 1934, he organized the Kisan Sabha. In 1934 he was elected from Poónch and Mirpur side as the member of legislation assembly. On Oct. 29, 1936, he tendered his resignation from the state assembly on the question of the grazing tax bill. The bill had been introduced in Jammu session in April 1936 where it was referred to the selected committee. No report was given by the selected committee and on 2 November 1936 Sardar Budh Singh submitted his resignation by his party from the Assembly which was accepted by Maharaja. He charged the Govt. with 'breach of faith' and said that it was of no use remaining a member of this Chamber.[19]

He met with the Hindus and Muslims of the state to organized a national level party of the State. This resulted in the formation of National Conference in 1939.[20] He was twice elected the president of the National Conference, first in 1942 and secondly in 1944. Sheikh Mohammad Abdullah called him the **father of the State**.[21]

Before Quit Kashmir Movement twice he was arrested and third time in quit Kashmir movement in 1946 he was an Inqulabi minded person and his slogan was **freedom** and **Inqulab**. After getting independence, he was a minister in Abdullah's Administration. Within two years, his portfolios were changed from relief and rehabilitation to health and then to information and broadcasting. Eventually he resigned from the Cabinet on October 14. 1950. It clearly indicated that he was a misfit in the politics of power.[22]

Politically also he felt somehow maladjusted. He was elected the first President of Provincial unit of the Jammu National Conference when it was formed. But he records in his anti biography that it hurt him when Sheikh Moh. Ahdullah accused him of **Suba-Parasti** (Regional Bias) in his role which Budh Singh could not bear and in 1953 he was against the activities of Sheikh Ahdullah and requested the State Government to arrest him.[23]

Ideologically, Budh Singh moved close to the communists. In a pamphlet entitled **'Communist Bogey'** in 1954, he cited reasons which attracted people to communism. He said, "The speed with which reforms are being introduced does not satisfy the poor, they want a revolution right now". In 1958 he isolated himself from the communist Movement also.[24]

He was the loneliest person in Kashmir politics who worked both for Hindus and Muslims. He breathed his last on May 23. 1975.[25]

Mr. Balraj Puri sums up his Bio-graphical note by saying, "with his crusading zeal, Courage of Conviction, radical views, capacity to under go hardships and firebrand eloquence, Budh Singh could he described as the father of the political unrest in J&K State. He raised his banner of revolt against the authoritarian monarchy long before any organized political party did so. With his non-sectarian and cosmopolitan out look he also sought to bridge cultural and regional diversities that bonded the State [26]

References

1. Mohammad Yassin, Freedom Struggle in Kashmir, p. 177.
2. Shastri R.N., Dogar Deya Char Namvar Shaksayat, Dogri Sansta, Jammu, p. 12.
3. Govt., J&K, Gen. Pol. Records, File No. 216/C-37 of 1920, p. 7.
4.. Shastri, R.N., op. cit., p. 12.
5. Sharma, B.P., Article in Kashmir Times, 1989, p. 5.
6. Govt., J&K.Pol.records, File:No.216/C-37 of 1920; p. 9.
7. Govt., J&K.Gen. Pol. Recrds, File No. 216 of 1921, p 5.
8. Mohammad Yassin, p. 178.
9. Govt., J&K.Gen. Pol. Deptt., File No. 216 of 1921, p 5.
10. Superintendent of Police Kashmir Province to 1.G.P. J&K State, 30. July 1920, J&K file No.216/c-37of 1920, p. 3.
11. *Ibid.*
12. Kour, Ravinderjeet, Political Awakening in Kashmir, pp. 42-43.
13. National Archives of India, Home Deptt. Pol. June 1972, F. No. 28 p. 5.
14. *Ibid.*
15. Govt. J&K Gen. Pol. Deptt. File No. 217 of 1925, p. 23;
16. *Ibid.*
17. Sharma, B.P., Article, Kashmir Times, 1989, p. 5.
18. *Ibid.*
19. Khan, G.H., Freedom Struggle in Kashmir, pp; 265-266.
20. Sharma. H Article. Kczshrnir Tinrs. 1989, p. 5.
21. *Ibid.*
22. Chabbra, G.S. & Charak. S.D.Jummu and Kashmir Aspects of Socio-Political theory. p. 54.
23. *Ibid.*
24. *Ibid.,* p. 55.
25. *Ibid.,* p. 56.
26. Mohammad Yassin. p. 181
27. *Ibid.,* & On the Road to New Kashmir, Note Book. Year 1957. p. 25.

Chapter - 6

Khilafat and Non-cooperation movement - Its Effect in Jammu Region

The growing indignation against the British rule led to the launching of the Khilaft and Non-Cooperation Movement.Turkey had faught against the British in the First World War. At the end of the war,Turkey which was one of the defeated countries, suffered injustices at the hands of Britian. In 1919, a movement was organized under the leadership of Mohamed Ali and Shaukat Ali, popularly known as Ali brothers,Abul Alam Azad , Hasrat Mohani and others to force the British government during the war and were released after it. The Khilafat committee which was set up to conduct this movement was joined by Gandhi ji. The Sultan of Turkey was also considered the Caliph or Khalifa, the religious head of the Muslims. The movement over the question of injustice done in Turkey was called the Khilafat Movement.[1]

The anti British nature of the Khilafat symbol was the common denominator in and other wise variegated movement. The Khilafat's other levels of meaning made it a symbol which could appeal to all strata of the muslim community. Jawahar Lal Nehru pointed out that "Khilafat" was related in the popular mind to the urdu word "KILAF", i.e. against. What even else it meant, the Khilafat called upon Indians to rally against the government.[2]

It gave a call for Non –Cooperation Movement in 1921. The movement on the Khilafat question soon merged with the movement against the repression in the Punjab and for swaraj.[3]

The movement was aimed at demonstration against the Rowlat Act, undoing the injustice done in Punjab and Turkey and attainment of Swaraj. This was followed by the boycott of legislatures. Most of the people refused to cast their votes and thousands of the students and lecturer boycotted their classes and jobs etc.

Khilafat and Non-Cooperation movement led its great effect on the northern part of the country especially on the Jammu region. It developed, some times along identical paths, but more often along parallel lines.

Khilafat Movement in Jammu

The Khilafat Movement in India, which spread almost allover Northern India in 1920, had a deep impact on the people of Jammu and Kahshmir.

In the Jammu region, which was situated in the close proximity of the Punjab, the Khilafat Movement evoked a widespread response. The most of the muslim aroused because of the religious appeal involved in the Khilafat and Hindus joined it because they considered[4] it a part of the struggle against the British.[5]

Despite the ban on political meetings in the state, some leading and influential persons persuaded Imams of various Mosques in Jammu to declare Jehad in their sermons after prayers, as was being all over India in connection with Khilafat Movement.[6]

Among the leaders of the Khilafat Movement in Jammu were Mohammad Yaqub, a petition writer, Rahmat-Ullah,

Mohammad Sayed an employee of the Home Minister, Detto Siraj from Gujranwalla, Qazi Zia Ullah, a retired Tehsildar, Rafi-ud-din, an employee of Home Minister's office, Tufail Mohammad, an employee of the Cooperative Bank, Ghulam Nabi, a clerk in the Court of Jammu, Rafi-ud-din, an employee in Anjurman Islamia etc.[7]

On 12March 1920 most of the Khilafat leaders attended the Friday prayers at the Mosque of Mohalla Qasban in Jammu. It was decided to consult Muslims like Pir Mitha Hafizullah and Moulvi Fida Mohammad an Imam of Mosque Mohalla Pathavan. Some of the leaders suggested that preachers should be invited from Punjab to deliver lectures on the Khilafat Movemnet.[8]

At a well-attended meeting on 13th March 1920, at the Islamic school Boarding House, Jammu it was resolved to observe a fast on Friday 19th March 1920, and to persuade the Muslims of Jammu to respond to the Central Khilafat Committee call for a hartal.6 On 17th March, 1920 a notice with the heading 'Jid-o-Jahad-Ke Akheri-Faisle-ki-Ghari' was pasted all over Jammu.[9]

The British Governor warned the chief organizers of the Khilafat Movement against disloyal or seditious speeches yet the Khilafat Movement continued unabated through out the winter.[10]

Non-Cooperation Movement in Jammu

Immediately after the massacre at Jalianwala Bagh, Martial Law was declared throughout the Punjab and a reign of terror spread everywhere.[11] The disturbances in Lahore and Amritsar and Gandhi s passive resistance movement against the Rowlatt-act aroused the indignation of the people in the Jammu and Kashmir State, especially in jammu, which was situated in the vicinity of Punjab.[12]

The Non-Cooperation and Satyagrah movement launched by congress under the leadership of Mahatma Gandhi in

1921, greatly inspired the people of Jammu region and made them conscious of the ideals of freedom and self rule.[13]

The impact of the satyagrah movement was felt on the students of college in Jammu. The students of the Prince Wales college were inflamed by the ideas of Non Coopertation movement and boycotted all authorities. They had also become possessed of the ideas that if all become one, one can be punished for any breach of discipline.[14]

On the 16Ih March 1921 hundreds of people went to Sialkot from Jammu in order to meet Mahatama Gandhi. Gandhi caps became common in Jammu, especially amongst students. One of the Lalä Lajpat Rai's notices calling on the students of all Colleges affiliated to the Punjab University to attend a non-cooperation meeting at Gujrawala on January 1921, was put up at the notice board of the Prince of Wales College, Jammu. A number of boys from the College hostel asked the Principal for permission to go to Gujranwala.[18] The Minister of Education acting on the orders of Government warned the students that the Maharaja was strongly averse to their participation in political demonstrations whose "Avowed object was to induce people to defy lawfully constituted authority".[15]

Despite the warning about 262 students attended the conference at Gujranwalla. The moving spirit was Prof. Daulat Ram and two students, Baldev Singh and Ishwar Dass.[16] The students shouted slogans such as **"Mahatama Gandhi, Ki Jai, Bande Mataram, Lala-Lajpat Rai Ki Jai, Mulana Bakshi Ki Jai, Robenson Ki Hai and College Ki Hai.** The situation became uncontrollable. The Government closed the Prince of Wales College and dismissed a number of students from the college.[17]

Pt Roop Krishan and Krishan Lal started to collect contributions for the Tilak Swaraj fund but it was banned by Maharaja and warning was also was given to them for future.

Throughout March 1922, a number of meetings were held in Jammu region. Speeches were made, exhorting the people to boycott foreign goods and use of Swadeshi clothes, cow protection, Hind- Muslim unity and abstention from liquor.[18]

Due to the personal intervention of Maharaja, the situtation did not take a serious turn as it had imagined. The state authorities turned out all the of the Non-Cooperation from the State.[19]

Speeches of a religious and political nature required prior permission of the Government.Advance copy of the speech had to be submitted. Special watch was kept over religious preachers.

The Arya Samaj also played an important role in the Jammu Non-cooperation Movement in Jammu. On 7th April,1921 prominent Arya Samaji's came from Gurkul, Hardwar, to deliver lectures.[20]

The Maharaja warned the president of Arya Samaj that no meeting would be allowed without permission and no speech should delivered on religious and political matters.[21]

The Muslims of Jainmu and Kashmir showed less enthusiasm to join the non-cooperation movement but once the Khilafat question was taken up the Khilafat Committee and the Congress, the Muslims joined the Non-cooperation agitation in a large number.

References

1. Govt. J&K Gen. Pol. Dept Files No.99/C, 1 March 1920, p. 5, and File No.200 of 1920, p. l.
2. Kaur, Ravinder, Political awakening in Kashmir, New Delhi, p. 91.
3. Govt. J&K Gen. Pol. Dept Files No.99/C, 1 March 1920, p. 5, and File No.200 of 1920, p. 7.
4. Govt. J&K Gen. Pol. Records Files No.101/C-i dated March 15, 1920, p. 1 4.
5. *Ibid.*, p. 32.

6. Govt. J&K Gen. Pol.Dept File No.101/C-March 16, 1920, p. 5.
7. Maulana Baksh to Chief Minister, Jammu J&K State, 17 March 1920, J&K Gen. Pol. Deptt File No.200 of 1920, p. 10 and File No.1 05/e/1 8 March 1920, p. 16.
8. Koul, Santosh, the freedom struggle in Jammu and Kashmir, p. 14, New Delhi, 1989.
9. Bannerman to Pol. Secy to Govt. of India in foreign and Pol. Department, 1" May 1919. National Archives of India, Home Department proceedings Pol. July 1919, No. 48.
10. Bannerman to Holland, 16th May, 1919, National Archive of India, Home Department Proceedings, Pol. July 1919, File No. 48, p. 32.
11. Daljit Singh, Chief Minister to Maula Baksh, Home Minister, J&K State, 29 January, 1921, J&K Pol. Deptt File No. 254-C of 1921, pp. 1 -14.
12. *Ibid.*
13. File No.180 of 1921, J&K Govt. Pol. Record. p. 32.
14. Bannerman to Jlhn Wood, 17" Feb., 1921, National Archives of India, Home Deptt Proceedings/ Pol. Jammu 1921, No. 12 p. 16 and File No.63/60 of 1921, p. 7.
15. FileNo. 63/60 of l92l, p. 5.
16. File No. 254/C of 1921, p. 5.
17. Principal of Prince Wales College, Jammu to Minister of Edu. J&K State, 1 Feb. 1921, File No.63/60-C of 192l, p. l2.
18. Windam to Thompson, 3rd April, 1922, National Archives of India, Home Deptt Proceedings, Pol. March 1922, F.No.18, p. 42.
19. Resident to S.P.O. Dennel, 13th Sept. 1922, National Archives of India, Home Deptt proceedings National Archives of India, Home Deptt proceedings P0 1923, File No.19 & *Ibid.,* p. 29.
20. File No. 157/C-11 of 1921, p. 19.
21. File No. 157/C-11 of 1921, p. 20.

Chapter - 7

World War-II and the Jammu Region

In World War-II whole world was engulfed in the war and caused social, political economic and moral destruction. Indians also involved in this war due to the British Government. Jammu and Kashmir State was not left behind, especially the Jammu region, which played a vital role and got number of decorations and. honours for the Jammu and Kashmir State.

Only few scholars have attempted to do general work on Jammu and Kashmir's involvement in World War-II, but they have not thrown ample light on the Jammu region's role in the World War-II. Earlier scholars did not do full justice with Jammu region, so conscious of the importance of this topic, I under took the study of the role of Jammu region in World War-II from 1939 to 1945.[1]

The peace that. was ushered in after World War-1st had always been an uneasy one. Although there was no war during the next 20 years, the threat had cropped up every now and then. The Germans had no difficulty accepting military defect but they had not accept the peace that was thrust upon them through the treaty of Versailles. Consequently the Germans had been on the look out for an opportunity to cut the shackles with which she had been bound by the treaty of Versailles. The rise of Nazism and emergence of Hitler made Germany a strong military power.[2]

The twenty years of peace were finally shattered when Germany invaded Poland on 1st September, 1939 and thus started the IInd World War. On one side were Germany, Italy and Austria known as axis powers, while the other side Britain, France and Russia were known as the Allies.[3] As the war progressed practically all the Countries of the world got engulfed in it and the war came to be known as IInd World War.[4]

The Viceroy in India without consulting political parties, declared India at war with Germany. The constitution was suspended. The so- called popular ministries in the state were dissolved over, this unilateral declaration of the Viceroy. The Indian National Congress, which was involved in a relentless struggle for independence was not ready to cooperate. They wanted a firm commitment from the British Government for granting independence after the war for cooperation and lending all help to the war efforts. However, it was clear that the Congress leaders did not regard this, an opportunity to prepare the people for a major assault on the British rule when it was at its weakest.[5]

The war actually broke out on 1st September, its imminence was fairly clear by 23 August as the British and French negotiations with Hitler headed for a dead-lock.[6] Reacting to the tense situation in Europe, His Highness, the Maharaja of Jammu and Kashmir sent the following telegram to His Excellency, the Viceroy of India on 24 August, "Last night's wireless ñéws sounded ominous, I hope I am wrong and the worse may yet be averted. But if not the whole empire must meet the resulting aggression on peace loving humanity and defend the sanctity of hearth and home and the cause of honour. I deprecate publicity and am loathe to speak personally but I do desire your Excellency and through you the kind emperor to know that if the war comes Jammu & Kashmir may be depended upon to do what Jammu &

Kashmir has ever done since coming under the aegis of his Britannical Majesty, and of course my personal services are always and will be, in the event of war, at His Majesty's disposal".[7]

Simultaneously, he placed two units of the state forces at the disposal of His Excellency, the Viceroy, and issued instructions to all officers and soldiers, who were on leave, to report to their respective units. The infantry battalions and batteries were kept in readiness to move at short notice.[8]

Maharaja's anticipatory action had been, so fast that the day after the war actually broke out, all the units of the state forces stood mobilized for war and in a state of readiness to march out a short notice. All these units were then placed at the disposal of the British Govt. He appealed to every Indian, "India must stand shoulder to shoulder with England in this hour of emergency. The settlement of their political difference must wait for the return of peace."[9]

Not more than two decades after the termination of the 1st World War, the people of Jammu region got another opportunity to prove their valour when the state forces mobilized to help the Allies in the IInd World War.[10]

Maharaja made an impassioned appeal to the Dogras in general and Rajputs in particular to help in the war effort by enrolling themselves in the army either in the state or the Indian army."[11] In order to induce his people to lend whole hearted support to the cause, his appeal was supplemented by the following proclamation issued by his Government,[12] "His Highness, Maharaja Bhadur with his unfailing regard for his subjects in general and Army in particular, has been graciously pleased to order that the officers and men of the units of his army who may be sent on active service shall continue to receive their pay and rations allowance from the state. As field rations and other field requirements are sure to be provided by the British Government. His Highness has ruled that the state shall not save the ration allowance but during the absence of the units from the state, pay that allowance to the families of those who are on an active service and such payments shall continue until the mobilized units remain on service out side the state to encourage the recruitment. He assured every one let every man who may here after enlist under His Highness "banner" realise that when he goes to fight at the bidding of his master, he does so as a soldier of a sovereign who will not only look after him while he is on the battle field, but also look after his family, and should he loose his life, his master will in the absence of the-bread winner not leave his family un-cared for."[13]

So far as those are concerned who are already serving in some unit or the other of His-Highness army, let themselves and their families take heart that the master who may order them to go and fight, will make it as his case to do all that is possible not to allow their families to suffer destitution or involved in object poverty.'[14]

The Maharaja in a message to his state forces conveyed to them, "you go attend by my good wishes. All the time you are away, you will be in my thought. I trust you to give a good account of your self, such an account as will add glory to the state and bring honour to your self, good luck and God be even with you."[15]

In order to give the proclamation wide publicity, one lakh copies of it were printed in Urdu. Of those 750 were distributed among the press correspondents, news papers, institutions and persons on the Government mailing list. While 73,000 and 26,000 copies were distributed in the region of Jammu and Kashmir respectively.'[16]

The response of the Maharaja's appeal was tremendous and right through the period of war there never was a dearth of recruits for not only the state forces but also the Indian army. This time the people of this region responded better than during the previous war, and nearly 51,000 recruits joined the army (Indian Army 45,000 state forces 6,000) up to the end of December, 1943.[17] By the end of the war total number of the recruits raised from Jammu region was about 55,000.[18] Considering the total population of Jammu region was a little Over 4,000,000 which included women, children, the old and infirm and a large section of the non-martial races not many able and young members of the fighting classes among the Dogras could have remained out of military service during the war.[19]

In response of these efforts more and more persons with higher physical standards came forward to join the army. They include the Sikhs, Gujjars and Jats as well.[20]

On September 1939, Jammu & Kashmir Praja Sabha Legislative Assembly, while endorsing the Maharaja's appeal resolved, "The Praja Sabha representing all classes, communities and interests in the state expresses its unflinching devotion to your Highness and support whole heartedly and unreservedly your Highness, determination to offer all the resources of the state, both in men and material, in the furtherance of the righteous cause, in which the armies of His Majesty, the king emperor are engaged, namely the cause of prevalence of right over might and of up holding the reign of law over brute forces."[21]

The Amar Sabha of Jammu through a telegram, offered their loyal and united service to His Highness in the conduct of the war. Some individuals too offered their services to the Maharaja for the righteous cause, whereas many pensioners offered their services without any extra emoluments.[22]

Similarly, the Wazir of Pôonch, through his telegram sought to convey the feelings of the citizens of Poonch. "Poonch people are eager for enlistment in India and state armies. Kindly wire number of Hindus and Muslims recruits required from Poonch for emergency and other recruitments. Poonch can supply over ten thousand recruits."

The Wazir of Poonch appealed to all the officers that they should offer their services to the Government at such a time of emergency. He declared that, "there is increasing need for Havaldars and Naibs to mobilize the people to join the army and to assist the recruiting staff at the recruiting centres. So all those who are retired or on leave should report to the recruitment drive."[23]

The working committee of the National Conference declared its support to the war efforts of the state Government but it also showed resentment over the special appeal made by the Maharaja to the Dogras and the Rajputs in the state to support the allied war efforts, ignoring rest of the people of the state. No doubt, the National Conference was justified in showing its resentment, as the appeal had been made only the Dogras and Rajputs of the State. According to them, the people of Kashmir too had every opportunity to contribute towards the war efforts of the state.[24]

The working committee of the National Conference. on 16th and 18th May 1942 issued following statement : At this juncture of the world history, it is right time that the people should realize the significance of the increasing danger to our country from the world's fascist forces. People must be roused from their apathetic attitude towards this war, which in the opinion of the working committee is no more a purely imperialistic conflict but has changed into peoples' front of the entire world against fascism and reaction, no matter that reaction is of, home made variety or of a foreign brand people of the State Kashmir too has every opportunity to contribute towards the war efforts of the State.[25]

In J & K, 1st JAK Mountain Battery, formed a part of the 5th Indian Division which was mobilized for service overseas, was under the command of Major (Late Lt. Col) Bhagwan Singh. It distinguished itself the conquest of entries particularly in the battle of Keren and capture of Asmara, as well as in the invasion of Syria, where it won a great battle honour on account of its gallant part in the attack on Jebel Mazar (Damascus).[26]

2nd J & K Mountain Battery and four infantry battalions served on the North Western frontier of India. After serving there for four years, the 4th JAK infantry was sent to Burma to join the 5th Indian division. There it earned great battle honour in the famous advance from Tiddim and in the attacks on Vital Corner, Kennedy Peak and Fort Whille.[27]

The Commander of the Division, with which the battery served, praised the standard of its efficiency under skilled command of Lt.Col. Bhagwan Singh. Similarly General Sir Claude-Acu-Chinleck, C-In-C of the imperial forces in the Middle East, conveyed his personal appreciation of the work of the battery to His Excellency Archibald Wavel, C-In—C of India (Late H.E., Lord Wavell, the Viceroy of India). Who, while adding his own appreciation, conveyed it to His Highness the Maharaja of Jammu & Kashmir. It's said, "Jammu & Kashmir-battery acquitted itself with great distinction in recent Damascus fightiig. Divisional command commands highly its steadiness under the enemies artillery, fire and the accuracy of its own fire supporting British infantry."[28]

Maharaja on receiving the message of appreciation felt elated and sent the ollowing appreciation message to Lt. Col. Bhagwan Singh of his heroic deeds: "Your Divisional Commander General Auchin-Leck and the C-In-C in India have expressed their appreciation of the work of yourself, your officers and their men in Damascus, remarked that you all acquitted yourself with great distinction I am most proud of you, and greatly value the fine example you set for your brother officers and men of all other units in the field, well done. My best wishes for your further success in thefuture."[29]

In recognition of the services of Lt. Col. Bhagwan Singh, the Maharaja on December 20, 1941, sanctioned a hereditary Jagir of Rs. 3,600 per annum in his favour which could be held by him and his male heirs in the direct line in perpetuity.[30]

On October 1, 1942 both the mountain batteries and the Artillery training centre were incorporated as permanent units with the Indian army.[31]

For conspicuous gallantry, while, serving on the various fields of the war, following decorations and honours were won by the valiant sons of this region:[32]

Decoration	No. of Decorations won
Victoria cross	one
Military cross	Five
Distinguished flying cross	one
Indian order of merit	two
Indian Distinguished service medals	fifteen
Member of the Br. Empire	seven
Military medals	Forty-One
Order of the Br. Empire (Military)	one
Order of the. Br. Indian	five
M.B.E (Military)	two.[33]

Impact of the war

(1) The people.of Jammu & Kashmir State were not really losers. They got unprecedented employment opportunities in both the state and Indian army, which helped them to raise their standard of life and widened their mental horizon.

(2) The demand of the Dogras in general and of the Dogra Rajputs in particular had vastly increased. Full recruiting facilities were provided to the Government of India.

(3) IInd World War brought huge financial crises on the Ex-Cheques of this poor state in this war, the defence expenditure of the state increased by more than 108 percent from Rs. 49, 16, 700 in 1938- 39 to Rs. 1,02,53,000 in 1945-46.

(4) The war aid committee was organized in July 1940 under the presidentship of Her Highness, the Maharanni Sahiba. The aim of the committee was to

collect funds in aid of the war. The war aid committee also established the "Trinket fund" the total contribution received by the committee till the end of February 1945 was Rs.9,87,3 15, which included Rs. 2,50,440 from the ruling family itself. Maharaja Hair Singh contributed the additional sum of Rs. 2,79,47 from his own privi purse.[34]

(5) The private individuals, revenue officers, Jagirdars and Lambardars hold public meetings to persuade the people to make contribution for war.

As a result of these efforts, by the middle of 1940, a sum of Rs.1,36,500 was collected.[35] During the war, the defence expenditure of the state increased by more than 108 percent from Rs. 49,16,700 in 1938-39 to Rs. 1,02,53,000 in 1945-46.[36]

The war years saw the scarcity of foodstuffs and other essentials of life demanded untiring efforts on the part of the leaders to prevent black marketing by unscrupulous dealers in these commodities. The war years also saw the growing importance of the Maharaj with the British Govt. He gave unstintéd help to, and placed all his resources at the disposal of the Govt. of India in this prosecution of the war. Any action that he would take against the people movement received support from the Imperial Government.[37]

References

1. Bamzai, P.N.K., Cultural and Political History of Kashmir, Vol. 3, M.D. Publications, Pvt. Ltd., New Delhi, p. 74.
2. Singh, Major, K. Brahma, History of Jammu & Kashmir Rifles (1820-1956), p. 173.
3. *Ibid.*
4. *Ibid.,* p. 220; Dhar, D.N, Dynamics of Political Change in Kashmir from Ancient to Modern Times, Krishna Publishers, New Delhi, p. 6l.
5. Dhar, D.N, Dynamics of Political Change in Kashmir from Ancient to Modern, Times, p. 67.

6. Singh, Major, K. Brahma, History of Jarnmu &-Kashrnir Rifles (i820-1956), p. 221.
7. G.O.I., P.D. (Pol Branch), File No. 40(12 - (5,) 39 of 1939, p. 54, crown file No. 287 (N.A.1.) War efforts ofJammu & Kashmir, J&K, Vol-2, No.3, Victory number, May-June, 1954, p. 9.
8. Jammu & Kashmir information, April-I944, p. 5; Administrative Report Jammu & Kashmir1938-39, *Ibid.*
9. G. 0.1, PD. (Pol. Branch)., File No; 40(12) - (5)39 of 1939, p. 54, Crown file No. 287 (N.A.1.) War efforts ofJammu & Kashmir, J&K, Vol. 2, No.3, Victory number, May-June, 1954, p. 9; The war, Maharaja of J&K, Personal appeal, Sept. 1939; p. 45.
10. *Ibid.*
11. The war, Maharaja of J&K, Personal appeal, Sep. 1939, p. 45.
12. Singh, Major, K. Brahma, History of Jammu & Kashmir Rifles (1820-1956), p. 121.
13. Administrative Report, J&K, 1938-39, pp. 210-215; Singh, Major, K. Brahma, History of Jammu & Kashmir Rifes (1820-1956), p. 121; Crown file no. 287, (N.A.I.), The War efforts of Jammu & Kashmir J.K.I, Vol. 2, No. 3, Victory No, May-June, p. 9. 14. Ibid.
15. Kapoor, M.L., Maharaja Hart Singh - 1895-1961, p. 92.
16. *Ibid.*
17. J.K.I., Vol. I, No. 1, April 1944, p. 7; and War efforts of Jammu & Kashmir State, J.K.I. Vol. 2, No. 3, May-June 1945, p. 9.
18. Saraf, Mulk, Raj, op. cit., p. 171.
19. Singh, Major, K. Brahma, History of Jammu & Kashmir Rifles (1820-1956), p. 121.
20. Kapoor, M.L, Maharaja Hari Singh 1895-1961, p. 92.
21. Praja Sabha Dabates, Sep. 18, 1939.
22. Adminitrative Reports 1938-1939,-315; and Kapoor, M.L., Maharaja Hari Singh (1895-96), p. 88.
23. Administrative Reports1940-41, p. 240.
24. Kapoor, M.L., Maharaja Hari Singh(1895-96),p. 88.
25. Dhar, D.N, Dynamics of Political Change in Kashmir from Ancient to Modern Times, p. 67.
26. Fortnightly Report of Kashmir Residency for the fortnight ending 31st January 1942-G.O.I.,F.P.D. File no. 9(9)-p of 1942, p-5; Crown File No. 287 (N.A.I.), p. 21; War efforts of Jammu

& Kashmir State, J.K.I, Vol. 2, No. 3, Victory number, May-June 1945, pp. 9-10/A Hand book of J&K State 1947-59.

27. Saraf, Mulk, Raj, op. cit., p. 72; Administrative report of the army dept.for sumbat 1997-97 (1940-41) A.D.D-1, Administrative report of the army dept. for sumbat 2000 (1943-44)A.D., p-1; Maharaja of Jaipur. File No. 63, pp. 66-67.
28. Kapoor, M.L., Maharaja Han Singh, (1895-96), p. 89.
29. *Ibid.,* p. 90.
30. *Ibid.*
31. Saraf Mulk Raj, op. cit, p. 171; Administrative report 1943-44, p-6; A Hand Book of Jammu & Kashmir State, F. J&K, Pub., 1947, p. 59.
32. War efforts of J&K State JKI, Vol L-2, No-3, May-June 1945, p-18; Saraf, Mulk Raj, Fifty years of Journalism, p. 72.
33. War efforts of Jammu & Kashmir State JKI, Vol. 2, No. 3, May-June 1945, p. 18; Saraf, Mulk Raj, op. cit., p. 174.
34. Kapoor, M.L., Maharaja Hari Singh 1895-96, p. 94.
35. Administrative report of J&K, 1944-45, p. 245/Kapoor, M.L., Maharaja Hari Singh, 1895-96, p. 95.
36. War efforts of Jammu and Kashmir State J.K.I. Vol. 2, No. 3, May-June 1954, p. 12; & G. Koul, G.E., Kashmir then and now-A Historical Survey, Srinagar, 1967, p. 108.
37. Bamzai, P.N.K, Cultural and political History of Kashmir pp. 740-74.

Biblography

A. Primary Sources

Archives-unpublished records

a. Indian National Archive Home and Foreign Deptt.

- File No. 9 of 1910.
- File No. 526 of 19ll.
- File No. 57/59 of 1917.
- File No. 30 of 1917.
- File No. 28 of 1917.
- File No. 39 of 1918.
- File No. 388/404 of 1918.
- File No. M 175 of 1918.
- File No. 14/33 of 1919.
- File No.9 of 1919.
- File No. 22/38 of 1921.
- File No 8 of 1922.
- File No. 19 0f 1923.
- File No. 39 of 1927.
- File No. 18 of 1931.
- File No. 423 of 1931.
- File No. 21 of 1939.
- File No. 67/ Part—II of 1946.
- File No. 59 of 1953.
- File No. 39 of 1954.

b. State Govt. Records:

- File No. 13/4 of 1904.
- File No. 117/p. 51 of 1904.
- File No. 46-5-18 of 1904.
- File No. 40-5-18 of 1904.
- File No.62 of 1904.
- File No. 131 of 1905.
- File No. 205/M-144 of 1906.
- File No. 30/1 of 1906.
- File No. 51/1-71 of 1906.
- File No. 164 of 1906.
- File No. 149 of 1906.
- File No. 99/N-102 of 1907.
- File No. 280 of 1909.
- File No. 43 of 1909.
- File No. 71/N/13/2 of 1909.
- File No. ISO/Part-lI of 1910.
- File No. 202/N-51 C of 1910.
- File No. 215 of 1910.
- File No. 49/P-33 of 1911.
- File No. 157/C of 1911.
- File No. 162 of 1912.
- File No. 238/P-47 of 1912.
- File No. 34 of 1912.
- File No. 254/P. 127 of 1912.
- File No. 242/P. 38 of 1912.
- File No. 27/45-C of 1913.
- File No. 418/PS-49 of 1913.
- File No. 91/P. 56 of 1913.
- File No. 69/2-1 06 of 1913.
- File No. 213/P. 106 of 1913.
- File No. 58/6-34 of 1913.

- File No.221/F-116 of 1913.
- File No. 204/2-159 of 1914
- File No. 71 of 1914.
- File No.33-9/C of 1914.
- File No. 57/38-C of 1916.
- File No.25/45-C of 1917.
- File No. 27/43-C of 1917.
- FileNo. 215 of 1917.
- File No. 61/P. 307 of 191 7.
- File No. 264/23 of 1917.
- File No.234/P. 53 of 1917.
- File No. 261/28 of 1917.
- File No.21/28-C of 1917.
- File No. 27/43-C of 1917.
- File No.61/P. 307 of 1918.
- File No. 262/77-C of 1918.
- File No.216/P. 92 of 1918.
- File No.213-P. 68 of 1918.
- File No. 23/31-C of 1919.
- File No. 125/40 of 1919.
- File No. 10/327 of 1919.
- File No.312/2-C of 1919.
- File No. 126/16N-C of 1919.
- File No.70/Jud. of 1919.
- File No. 72/JLE of 1919.
- File No.69/N-E of 1919.
- File No. 39/2 of 1919.
- File No. 265/129 of 1920.
- File No. 225/129 of 1920.
- File No. 229 of 1920.
- File No. 209 of 45-C of 1920.
- File No. 99/C-I of 1920.

- File No. 216/C-37 of 1920.
- File No. 200/C of l920.
- File No.104/1-C of 1920.
- File No.354/C of l920.
- File No. 121 of 1920.
- File No. 162 of 1921.
- File No. 157 of 1921.
- File No.63/60-C of l921.
- File No. 254/C of 1921.
- File No. 180 of 1921.
- File No. 73/97-C of l921.
- File No. 261/28 of 1921.
- File No. 162 of 1922.
- File No. 55 of 1922.
- File No.386/P. 33 of 1923.
- File No.267/P. 57 of 1923.
- File No.396-M of 1923.
- File No. 72/JLF of 1924.
- File No. 97/63-g of 1924.
- File No.93/63-g of 1924.
- File No. 334 of 1925.
- File No. 217 of 1925.
- File No.57/38-C of 1926.
- File No. J-31 of 1927.
- File No. 259/5-32 of 1930.
- File No. 326 of 1930.
- File No. 417/5-23 of 1931.
- File No. 13/23 of 1931.
- File No.418/PS-149 of 1931.
- File No. 13/14 of 1931.
- File No. 261/5-2 of 1931.
- File No. 327 of 1931.

- File No. 12 of 1931.
- File No. l8 of 1931.
- File No. 138/2 of 1931.
- File No. 167/29 of 1931
- File No. 18 of 1931.
- File No. 423 of 1931.
- File No. 479 of 1931.
- File No. 485 of 1931.
- File No. 474 of 1931.
- File No. 80/1 0-G of 1931.
- File No. 93/10 0f 1931.
- File No. 86/104 of 1931.
- File No. 84 of 1931.
- File No. 167/129 0f 1931.
- File No.PS-298/12 of 1931.
- File No. 94 of 1932.
- File No. 134/43 of 1932.
- File No. 156/ 8-5 of 1932.
- File No. 92 of 1932.
- File No. 90/39 of 1 932.
- File No. 99 of 1932.
- File No. 190/ 292 of 1932.
- File No. 416/72 of 1932.
- File No. 194/104 of 1932.
- File No. 208/217 of 1932.
- File No. 297/88 of 1932.
- File No. 6671PS-579 of 1932.
- File No.232II-PAS of 1932.
- File No. 109 of 1932.
- File No 94 of 1932.
- File No. 200 /194 of 1932.
- File No. 192 1PS-169 of 1932.

- File No. 298 of 1932.
- File No. 402123 of 1932.
- File No. 420 of 1932.
- File No. 422 of 1932.
- File No. 2671P. 579 of 1932.
- File No. 390/44 of 1932.
- File No. 418/82 of 1932.
- File No. 487 1PS-88 of 1932.
- File No. 208/217 of 1932.
- File No. PS-190/292 of 1932.
- File No. 135 1PS of 1932.
- File No. 59 of 1933.
- File No. 481 / PS-49 of 1933.
- File No. 13/ 10-A of 1934.
- File No. 51/1-27of 1936.
- File No. 41 /P.J.S of 1937.
- File No. 31 /D-6 of 1937.
- File No. 1 74/D-37 of 1937.
- File No. 44/D-15 of 1937.
- File No. 128/B-446/38 of 1938.
- File No. 129 /B-44 of 1938.
- File No. 390 of 1938.

c. Govt Unpublished Records

1. His Highness Messages to His Believed People 9th July, 1931.
2. Stormy demonstrations in Jammu, Kashmir Bureau of Information, New Delhi.
3. Jammu and Kashniir Constituent Assembly opening address by Hon'ble S.M. Abdullah, Srinagar. November 3rd, 1951, printed at Caxton Press, New Delhi.
4. Revised List of Ruling Princes Chief and leading personage of the J & K State of Gilgit Agencies.

5. Unanimous Vote of Confidence in Bakshi Government Ranbir Govt., Press, Jammu.
6. The Flag Issue by Kashmir Bureau of Information, New Delhi.
7. India and Kashmir (Constitutional Aspect).
8. Kashmir Appeal to World Conference by S.M. Abdullah, Ranbir Press.
9. Kashmir— A Glorious Valley by J.L Nehru, 1939, New Delhi.
10. Jammu situation an objective analysis by S.M. Abdullah by Ranbir Press.
11. Report Book-On the Road of New Kashmir, New Delhi.
12. Sir Ganga Ram Report, State Archive Repository, Jammu.
13. Report by L. W. Jardine, LCS, Special Minister on the measures adopted for the restoration of law and order in Mirpur Wazarat and Rajouri Tehsil.
14. Report on an inqufry into disturbance at Jammu and its environment during first week of November 1931 conducted by L. Middleton LCS.
15. His Highness Govt Jammu and Kashmir — Orders on the Recommendations Contained III the Glancy Commission's Report.
16. Report of the Commission appointed under the orders of His Highness the Maharaja Bahadur dated the 12th November 1931 to enquire into grievances and complaints.
17. His Highness Govt Jammu and Kashmir Evidence Recorded in Republic by the Srinagar Riots Enquiry Committee.
18. Documents relating to Poonch State Archive Jammu.
19. Report - Five months issued by Directorate of Information and Broadcasting, Jammu and Kashmir state.

20. A note on Jammu and Kashmir State - 1928, Ranbir Press, Jammu.
21. Report - Kashmir Averts National Disaster (Bakshi Gulam Mohammad Call to People).
22. A Report-Jammu and Kashmir Regional Autonomy, Mehra off-set Press, New Delhi.
23. Sadar-i-Riyst, Address to Legislative Assembly. Jammu, 24 March, 1954.

d. Hand Books

1. A Hand Book of J&K State. Govt Publications, Ranbir Govt Press.
2. A Hand Book of J&K Govt J&K Administrative Reports, Ranbir Press, 1945.
3. A Hand Book - Jammu and Kashmfr Operations 1947-48, Questions and Answers, Himalayan Books, New Delhi.
4. A Hand Book of J&K State, 1947-1959, An account of activities of first three years of Sheikh Abdullah's Govt. Printed at Ranbir Press, Jammu 1951.
5. A Hand Book of J&K State, Jammu situation (an objective analysis) Published by Kashmir Bureau of Information, New Delhi and Printed at Caxton Press, New Delhi.
6. A Hand Book of J&K State Praja Parishad Movement in Jammu, A STAB in India's Back by Piyar Singh by National Publishing House, Jammu.

e. Administration Reports

1. A. R. Year 1930-31.
   A. R. Year 1932-33;
   A.R. Year 1933-35
   A.R. Year 1936-37
   A.R. Year 1939-40
   A.R. Year 1943-44

A.R. Year 1944-45

A.R. Year 1946-49

A.R. Year 1949-50.

A.R Year 1951-52.

A. R. Year 1952-53.

A.R. Year 1953-54

A.R. Year 1954-55

A.R. Year 1955-56

2. Part-Il. 26th March to 8th April, 1936
3. Vol. V, Part-I Sixth to 17 Oct. 1936, 5 session.
4. Vol. VI, 6th April, 1937, Sixth session.
5. Vol. VI, Part-V, 14th April, 1937, Sixth session.
6. Vol. VI, Part-X, 22nd April, 1937, Sixth session.
7. Vol. VI, Part-XI, 22nd April, 1937, Sixth session.
8. Vol. VI, Part-XII, 27th April, 1937, Sixth session.
9. Vol. VI, Part-XV, 29th April, 1937, Sixth session.

g. Assembly Debates

Vol. I, II, III of 1935.

Vol. IV of 1936 Part-I.

Vol. IV of 1936 Part-Il.

Vol. VI of 1937.

h. Commission Reports

1. Report of the Jammu and Kashmir Commission of Inquiry (1967).
2. Report of the Jammu and Kashmfr Commission of Inquizy (1972).
3. Annual Bulletin of Vital Statistics Govt. of Jammu and Kashmir, 1987.

i. Pamphlets

1. Plea for State Subject, Definition and Genesis, by Dogra Sadhar Sabha.

2. Article 370 and Regional Autonomy, Balraj Puri, (Jammu N.D).
3. One Day Convention of Jammu Maha Sabha: A Report, Jammu Mahasabha (Jammu N.D).
4. A Ringing Call for Sanity Goodwill and Communal Unity Jammu, Maha Sabha (Jammu N.D).
5. Jammu Discontent- Causes and Cures, Balraj Puri, Delhi, 1967.
6. Birth Pages of New Kashmir By N.S. Phalke, Published by Ranbir Press.

j. Census Reports

1. Census 1911, K, Part-I Vol. XX.
2. Census 1921, K, Part-I, Vol. XXII.
3. Census 1921, K, Part-land II, Vol. XXIV
4. Census of India, 1931, J&K State, Part-I.
5. Census 1931, J&K, Part-Il.
6. Census of India 1941, J&K State, Part-I and IL

k. Manuscripts

1. Wazir Ganga Nath, "A Report on the Administration of Jammu and Kashmir State", 1942, Jammu Archieve.

l. Journals:

1. Bharatiya Jana - Sangh 'Kashmir Problem and Jammu Satyagraha, an Objective Study'. New Delhi (N.D.).

m. Letters:

Pt Prem Nath Dogra's Letter to the Minister of Revenue and Agriculture, Govt of Jammu and Kashmir, 9th April, 1932, Available from family sources.

B. Secondary Sources

a. Articles

1. Facing Internal Threats to nations integrity, www.Hindu.Book/ Org/Vision.
2. Dhar, Trilokinath, A story of Kashmir Affair-A keep into the past, Kashmir Samachar, Articles on Politics.
3. Bhasin, Yash, Pt Prem Nath Dogra: A man of Commitment and conviction, Daily Exceissior, (N.D.).
4. Dogra Durga Dass, Pt Prem Nath Dogra, Panorama, Jammu
5. Socio-Reilgious Activities of the Arya Samaj and Kashmir state, Maharshi Dayanand University Research Journal (Acts), Vol. 3, Numbers, 1988, p. 43.

b. Praja Sabha Debates

1. Vol. IV, Part-I, 16th to 25th March, 1936, 4th session.

c. Newspapers:

1. Chandin Urdu (1940-1961).
2. Ranbir in Urdu (1919-1952).
3. The Dogra Gazette in Urdu (1932-1953).
4. Khalid, Srinagar.
5. Martand, Srinagar.
6. Hamdard, Srinagar.
7. Kidmat, Srinagar.

11. Daily Excelsior.
12. The Kashmir Times.
13. Hindustan Times.
14. The Times of India.
15. Indian Express.
16. Forum/Bombay.
17. Kashmir Samachar.
18. Panorama.

d. Magazines

Janata, Vol. XXII, March 1978.

e. Interview:

1. B.P.Sharma.
2. O.P.Shastri.

f. Thesis and Dissertations

1. Bharham, K., Political Agitation in Kashmiri 1931 and emergence of Muslim Conference, Dissertation, History Deptt., Jammu.
2. Kumar, Sudarshan, Social History of Jammu City, From 1885 to 1947 A.D., Dissertation, History Deptt., Jammu.
3. Ganesh, Goswami, Beggar System in Jammu and Kashmir, Dissertation, History Deptt., Jammu.
4. Edison, David 1982, 'Sher-i-Kashmir: A lion of Kashmir, Sheikh Abdullah and Dispute over relationship between J&K State and the Indian Union, University Microfilms, International Annarb-our Michigan U.S.A., London, thesis.
5. Gupta, Kishore Lal, Social History of Jammu Province from 1901-1961. Thesis, 1984, History Deptt,. Jammu.
6. Bala, Renu, Regional Political Parties and Constitutional Developments of Jammu and Kashmir — A Study of Praja Parishad — 1999. Dissertation, Pol. Science Deptt., Jammu.
7. Jamwal, Anjana Rani, Issue and aspiration in Jammu region: A Political Profile 1999, Dissertation, Political Science Deptt., Jammu.
8. Kapoor, M.L., Social, Economic History of Jammu and Kashmir State, 1885-1925, Thesis, History Deptt., Jammu.

g. Books

1. Anand, A.S., The constitution of Jammu and Kashmir: Its Development and Contents, Second edition and third edition, Delhi Universal Law Publishing, New Delhi. 1994, 1998.
2. Anand, A.S., The Development of Constitution of Jammu and Kashmir, Light and Life Publishers, New Delhi, 1980.
3. Andrew and Mukerjee, Rise and Growth of Congress in India, Meenakshi Prakashan, Meerut, 1967.
4. Aggarwal, J.C., S.P., Modern History of Jammu and Kashmir Vol. I and II Ancient Times to Shimla Agreement, New Delhi, 1995.
5. Akbar, M.I. India - The Seige, Penguin, New Delhi,1985.
6. Bazaz, P.N., Struggle for Freedom in Kashmir, Kashmir Publishing, Srinagar, 1954.
7. Bazaz, P.N., Inside Kashmir, Kashmir Publishing, Srinagar, 1951.
8. Banizai, P.N.K., A History of Kashmir, Metropolitan, New Delhi, 1966.
9. Bamzai, P.N.K., A History of Kashmir— Political, Social and Cultural from the Earliest to the present date, New Delhi, 1962.
10. Bamzai, P.N.K., Cultural and Political History of Kashmir, Vol.3, Modern Kashrnir; D. Publications, 1994.
11. Bhat, Koul, Ram Krishan, Political and Constitutional Development of the Jammu and Kashmfr Seema Publications, New Delhi, 1989.
12. Bhattacharjea, Ajit, Kashmir- The Wounded Valley, UBS Publishers and Distributors Ltd., New Delhi, 1994.
13. Bose, Sumantra, The Challenge in Kashmir — Democracy Self Determination and a Just Peace, Sage Publication, New Delhi, 1997.

14. Bakshi, S.R., SheiKh Mohammad Abdullah, Book House, Jammu, 1995.

15. Bushan, D.R., Vidhy, State Politics and Govt Jammu and Kashmir, House, Jammu, 1964.

16. Biscoe, C.E., Tyndali — Kashmir in see light and Shade, London, 1922.

17. Charak, Sukhdev Singh, History and Culture of Himalayan States - Jammu and Kashmir, Light and Life, New Delhi, 1983.

18. Chowhan, Amar Singh, Development of Education in the Jammu and Kashmir State, Atlantic Publishers and Distributors, New Delhi, 2001.

19. Charak, Sukhdev Singh, Histography of Jammu, Book House, Jammu, 1997.

20. Das, Durga, SardarPatel's Correspondence, 1945-50, Vol. 1, Nav Jivan Publishing House, Ahmedabad, 1971.

21. Dhar, Trilokinath, History of Kashmir— A key into the past, Kashmir Samachar, Article in politics in Kashmir, Kashmir Information Com./Kash-Sam Kashmir Affairs, 2002.

22. Fazili, Manzoor, Socialist Ideas and Movements in Kashmir, 1919-1947, Gulshan Publication,Srinagar, 1982.

23. Gupta, Sisar, Kashmir— A Study of India-Pakistan Relations, Ana Publishing House, Bombay, 1956.

24. Hussain, Majid, Geography of Jammu and Kashmir, Rajesh Publications, New Delhi, 1987.

25. Hasnin, N., Hindu, Muslim Relation, A Publishing Corporation, New Delhi, 1996.

26. Handa, R.L., Freedom Struggle in Princely State, New Delhi, 1989.

27. Koul, Santosh, Freedom Struggle in Jammu and Kashmir, Anmol Publications, New Delhi, 1990.

28. Koul, Pt Anand, Geography of Jammu and Kashmir State, Life Publishers, New Delhi, 1978.
29. Khan G.H., Freedom Struggle in Kashmir 1931-1940, Light and Life Publishers, New Delhi, 1980.
30. Koul, Kachru, Shyam, Omkar, Jammu, Kashmir and Ladakh Ringside Views, Shyog Prakashan, New Delhi, 1998.
31. Kapur, M.L., Maharaja Hari Singh 1895-1961, Har Anand Publications, Delhi, 1989.
32. Kour, Ravinderjeet, Political Awakening in Kashmir, APH Publishing Corporation, New Delhi,1992.
33. Koul, G.L., Kashmir Then and Now - A Historical Survey, Publishing House, Srinagar, 1969.
34. Koul, Bhatt, Prem Krishan, Political and Constitutional Development of Jammu and Kashmir, Seema Publications, Delhi, 1990.
35. Kapur, M.L., History of Jammu and Kashmir state, Kashmir History Publications, Jammu, 1990.
36. Koul, S.N., Dynamics of Kashmir Politics, Ranjit Publications, New Delhi, 2001.
37. Kak, B.L., Kashmir Problems and Politics, Seema Publications, Delhi, 1981.
38. Kamble, J.R., Rise and Awakening of Depressed Classes in India, New Delhi, 1979.
39. Lamb, Alastair, Arisen in Kashmir, Delhi, 1967.
40. Modhok, Balraj, Bungling in Kashmir, New Delhi, 1974.
41. Modhok Balraj, Kashmir Centre of NewAlignments, Deepak Prakashan, New Delhi, 1963.
42. Modhok, Balraj, Jammu Kashmir Ladakh Problem and Solution, Reliance Publishing House, New Delhi, 1987.
43. Mahajan, Hari Om, A study in the spread of Education and Consciousness, 1857-1925, New Delhi, 1980.

44. Mahajan, Hari Om, Beyond the Kashmir Valley, Har Anand Publications, New Delhi, 1998.
45. Mujumdar, R. C., History of Freedom Movement in India, Vol. III, Delhi, 1969.
46. Naqash, Shah, Nasir A., G.M., Kashmir from Crises to Crises, ADM Publishing Corporation, New Delhi. 1997.
47. Puri, Balraj, Simmering Valcano: A Study of Jammu's Relation with Kashmir, Sterling, New Delhi, 1981.
48. Puri, Balraj, Jammu — A dice to Kashmir — angle, New Delhi, 1966.
49. Puri, Balraj, Jammu and Kashmir Triumph and Tragedy of Indian Federalisation, Sterling, New Delhi, 1981.
50. Pannnikar, K.M., Foundation of Kashmir State, London, 1930. –
51. Philips, C.H., Evolution of India and Pakistan Documents, New Delhi, 1991.
52. Raghvan, G.S., The Warning in Kashmir, Jay Kay Book House, Jammu, 1993.
53. Raghvan, G.S., The Working of Kashmir, Pioneer Press, Allahabad, 1931.
54. Risky, Scitterbert, The People of India, London,1908.
55. Rai, Lajpat, A Histoiy of Arya Samaj, An Account of its origin, doctrines and activities with a biographical sketch of account of its origin, Calcutta, 1967.
56. Sharp, M., A note on education in the state of Jammu and Kashmir, Calcutta, 1916.
57. Singh, Karan, Sadar-i-Riyst: An Autobiography, Vol. 2, 1953-67, Oxford University Papers, New Delhi, 1985.
58. Singh, Karan, Sadar-i-Riyst: An Autobiography, Oxford University Press, New Delhi, 1982.

59. Saraf Muhammad Yusaf, Kashmir's Fight for Freedom, Vol. 12, 1931-46, 1947-48, Kashmir History Committee Edition, Lahore, 1977, 1979.
60. Singh, Lt Co. Bhagwan, Political Conspiracies of Kashmir, Light and Life Publishers, New Delhi, 1973.
61. Shastri, R.N., Dogra Deya Char Namvar Shaksayat Dogri Sanstha, Jammu, 1969.
62. Shah, Gulshan, State Subjectship in Jammu and Kashmir, Mis Jupitor, Srinagar, 1938.
63. Sexana, H.L., Tragedy of Kashmir, Nationalist Publishers, New Delhi, 1975.
64. Saraf, M.R., Jeewan Chariter, Sher-i-Dugar, LaIa Hansraj, 1886-1944, Jammu, 1907.
65. Saraf, M.R., Fifty Years as a Journalist, New Delhi, 1947.
66. Singh, Justice Jaswant, Jammu and Kashmir Political and Constitutional Development, Har Anand Publications, 1996.
67. Singh, Maj K. Brahma, Retd, History of Jammu International, New Delhi, 1990.
68. Singh, Narinder, Political Awakening in Kashmir, M.K. Publishers, Delhi, 1989.
69. Shahdari, Naveen, The Arya Samaj Hindu without, Hinduism, Vikas Publishing House, Delhi, 1972.
70. Singh, Nirmal Kumar, Inter-Communal Relations in Jammu and Kashmir, Book House, Jammu, 1989.
71. Sharma, S.P., Heritage of Jammu and Kashmir and Ladakh, Radha Publications, New Delhi, 2001.
72. Sharma, S.P., HerItage of Jammu and Kashmir and Ladakh, Radha Publications, New Delhi, 2001.
73. Saraf Mulk Raj, Shar-a-Dogra-Lala Hans Raj, 1866-1947, Raj Mehal Publishers, Jammu, 1984.
74. Schofield, Victoria, Kashmir in the Crossfire, Published Vinod Vasistha for Viva Books, 1997.

75. Teng, M.K., State Government and Political Jammu and Kashmir, Anmol Publications, New Delhi, 1998.
76. Teng, M.K., Kashmir Myth of Autonomy, Anmol Publications, New Delhi, 1998.
77. Thakur, K.T. Harigh, Alienation and Integration in Jammu and Kashmir, Jaipur, 1999.
78. Teng, Koul, Mohan, Krishan, Santosh, Kashmir's Special Status, Oriental Publishers, Delhi, 1975.
79. Teng, Koul, Ram Krishan, Kashmir Constitutional History and Documents, New Delhi, 1977.
80. Teng, Mohan Krishan, Kashmir Article 370, Anmol Publications, New Delhi, 2001.
81. Vaid, Dr S.P., How Partition Rocked Jammu and Kashmir, Shyama Publications, Jammu, 2002.
82. Verma, P.S., Jammu and Kashmir, the Publishing House, New Delhi, 1994.
83. Vidya Bhushan - State Politics and Government in Jammu and Kashmir, Book House, Jammu, 1985.
84. Yassian, Mohammad, History of Freedom Struggle in Jammu and Kashmir, Life and Light Publishers, New Delhi, 1980.
85. Wadhwa, Dr K.K., Constitutional Autonomy - A case study of J&K, Bhavana Books and Prints, New Delhi, 1993.
86. Zutshi, U.K., Emergence of Political Awakening in Kashmir, New Delhi, 1986.

Appendices

Name of the Bodies/ Associations1'individuals who Submitted Written Memorandums to the Commission in 1967-1968

Shri Abdul Aziz Shawl, Ex-MLA, P.O. Rajouri
All J&K Backward Classes Union, Jammu
All J &K Christian Association, Jammu
All J&K National Integration Front, Jammu
Anjuman Islamia, Jammu
Shri Bansi Lal Kohistani, Jammu
Beopar Mandal, Jammu
Bharatiya Depressed Classes League, Jammu
Congress Committee, Rajouri
District National Congress Committee, Udhampur
Dogra Mandal, Jammu
Dogra United Front, Jammu
Ex-Officers of the J&K Forces who retired before 1957, Jammu
Ex-Servicemen of J&K State, Jammu Sofi Ghulam Ahmed Gash, Srinagar
Gujar Samaj Sudhar Sabha, Poonch District

Jammu Autonomy Forum

Jammu Citizen's Council, Jammu

Janta Adhikar Raksha Samiti, Jammu

J&K Agriculturists Association, Jammu.

Jammu and Kashmir Ravidas, Sabha, Jammu

J&K Shia United Front, Srinagar

Jammu and Kashmir State Gujar Samaj Sudhar Sabha,

Jammu, Jammu and Kashmir Students Congress (Shri K. Sharma)

Jammu and Kashmir Students Congress (Shri Preetam Singh) Shri J.R. Sethi of Jammu

Jat Sudhar Sabha, J&K State, Jammu S/Shri Jivan Ram and Chabital Kapoor of Village Chakcharat Ram, Baramullah.

Kisan Conference Doda, Jammu

Nehru Ekata Committee, Jammu

Praja Socialist Party, Jammu and Kashmir State, Jammu

Shri Khurshi Anwar Dogra, Jammu

Shri Mela Ram, Advocate, Jammu

Shri Mohan Lal Motial, Jammu

Shri Mulk Raj Acharya, Jammu

Secretary, Naya Bhawan, Jammu

Shri Guru Singh Sabha Jammu, Akali Dal Jammu Province

"Uprooted Muslims of Tehsil Ramnagar, District Udhampur (Jammu)"

Zamindara Association, Jammu;

Anjuman Islamia, Jammu

Beopar Mandal, Jammu Dogra Mandal, Jammu

Dogra, United Front, Jammu,

Ex-J&K Militia Personnel, Jammu,

Ex-serviceman of J&K State, Jammu

J&K Agriculturists Association, Jammu,

Appendices 211

Janta Adhikar Raksha Samiti, Jammu,

Jat Sudhar Sabha, J&K State, Jarnmu,

Pradesh Congress Refugee Advisory Committee, Jammu,

Shri Guru Singh Sabha Jammu, Akali Dal Jammu

Province, and Sikh Minority Board, Jammu and Kashmir, Jammu,

Sharnarthi Action Committee, Jammu, Sharnarthi

Pratinidhi Board, Jammu,

Zamindara Association, Jammu

The Jammu and Kashmir State Gujar Samaj Sudhar Sabha Jammu

Shri Guru Singh Sabha, Jammu and Kashmir, The Sikh Minority Board

Sikh Riyasati Akali Dal, Jammu

Zamindara Association, Jammu

Agriculturists Association, Jammu

Janta Adhikar Raksha Samiti, Jammu

Anjuman Islamia, Jammu

Jammu Citizens Council, Jammu

Praia Socialist Party, Jammu and Kashmir State, Jammu

Shri Phulel Singh, Doda.

All J&K National Integration Front, Jammu.

All J&K Backward Classes Union, Jammu

J&K Ravidas Sabha, Jammu

Shri Prabhu Shoor, Village Kangri, Distt. Rajouri

Jat Sudhar Sabha, Jammu and Kashmir State, Jammu

All J&K Kshatriya Sadar Sabha, Jammu

Dogra Kashtriya Sadar Sabha, Jammu

Khukhran Bradri (Kashatriya Khukhran), Jammu

Beopar Mandal, Jammu

Convener, Pradesh Congress Refugee Advisory Committee, Jammu

Chairman, Public Service Commission, Jammu

Chief Secretary: Commission, Planning

Development, Jammu

Finance Secretary: Food Commissioner; Revenue Secretary Jammu and Additional Secretary, Education, Jammu

Shri G. L. Dogra, Minister of Revenue

Tribute to the Students

Martyrs of 17th and 18th October, 1966.

In the Loving Memory of the Students killed on 17th and 18th October, 1966.

Index

परशुराम की प्रतीक्षा

परशुराम की प्रतीक्षा

रामधारी सिंह 'दिनकर'

लोकभारती प्रकाशन

लोकभारती प्रकाशन
पहली मंजिल, दरबारी बिल्डिंग, महात्मा गांधी मार्ग
प्रयागराज-211 001
वेबसाइट : www.lokbhartiprakashan.com
ईमेल : info@lokbhartiprakashan.com

शाखाएँ : 1-बी, नेताजी सुभाष मार्ग, दरियागंज
नई दिल्ली-110 002
अशोक राजपथ, साइंस कॉलेज के सामने
पटना-800 006
1, अनमोल सोराबजी संतुक लेन, धोबी तलाव,
मरीन लाइंस, मुम्बई-400 002

पहला संस्करण : 1963
इक्कीसवाँ संस्करण : 2025

मूल्य : ₹ 395

यश प्रिंटोग्राफिक्स
नोएडा-201 301 (उत्तर प्रदेश)
द्वारा मुद्रित

PARSHURAM KI PRATIKSHA
Pomes by Ramdhari Singh 'Dinkar'

ISBN : 978-81-85341-13-2

दो शब्द

प्रथम संस्करण

इस संग्रह में कुल अठारह कविताएँ हैं, जिनमें से पन्द्रह ऐसी हैं जो पहले किसी भी संग्रह में नहीं निकली थीं। केवल तीन रचनाएँ 'सामधेनी' से लेकर यहाँ मिला दी गई हैं। यह इसलिए कि इन कविताओं का असली समय अब आया है।

नेफ़ा-युद्ध के प्रसंग में भगवान् परशुराम का नाम अत्यन्त समीचीन है। जब परशुराम पर मातृ-हत्या का पाप चढ़ा, वे उससे मुक्ति पाने को सभी तीर्थों में घूमते फिरे, किन्तु, कहीं भी परशु पर से उनकी वज्रमूठ नहीं खुली यानी उनके मन से पाप का भान नहीं दूर हुआ। तब पिता ने उनसे कहा कि कैलास के समीप जो ब्रह्मकुंड है, उसमें स्नान करने से यह पाप छूट जाएगा। निदान, परशुराम हिमालय पर चढ़कर कैलास पहुँचे और ब्रह्मकुंड में उन्होंने स्नान किया। ब्रह्मकुंड में डुबकी लगाते ही परशु उनके हाथ से छूटकर गिर गया अर्थात् उनका मन पाप-मुक्त हो गया।

तीर्थ को इतना जाग्रत् देखकर परशुराम के मन में यह भाव जगा कि इस कुंड के पवित्र जल को पृथ्वी पर उतार देना चाहिए। अतएव, उन्होंने पर्वत काटकर कुंड से एक धारा निकाली, जिसका नाम, ब्रह्मकुंड से निकलने के कारण, ब्रह्मपुत्र हुआ। ब्रह्मकुंड का एक नाम लोहित-कुंड भी मिलता है। एक जगह यह भी लिखा है कि ब्रह्मपुत्र की धारा परशुराम ने ब्रह्मकुंड से ही

निकाली थी, किन्तु, आगे चलकर वह धारा लोहित-कुंड नामक एक अन्य कुंड में समा गई। परशुराम ने उस कुंड से भी धारा को आगे निकाला, इसलिए, ब्रह्मपुत्र का एक नाम लोहित भी मिलता है। स्वयं कालिदास ने ब्रह्मपुत्र को लोहित नाम से ही अभिहित किया है। और जहाँ ब्रह्मपुत्र नदी पर्वत से पृथ्वी पर अवतीर्ण होती है, वहाँ आज भी परशुराम-कुंड मौजूद है, जो हिन्दुओं का परम पवित्र तीर्थ माना जाता है।

लोहित में गिरकर जब परशुराम का कुठार पाप-मुक्त हो गया, तब उस कुठार से उन्होंने एक सौ वर्ष तक लड़ाइयाँ लड़ीं और समन्तपंचक में पाँच शोणित-ह्रद बनाकर उन्होंने पितरों का तर्पण किया। जब उनका प्रतिशोध शान्त हो गया, उन्होंने कोंकण के पास पहुँचकर अपना कुठार समुद्र में फेंक दिया और वे नवनिर्माण में प्रवृत्त हो गए। भारत का वह भाग, जो अब कोंकण और केरल कहलाता है, भगवान् परशुराम का ही बसाया हुआ है।

लोहित भारतवर्ष का बड़ा ही पवित्र भाग है। पुराकाल में वहाँ परशुराम का पाप-मोचन हुआ था। आज एक बार फिर लोहित में ही भारतवर्ष का पाप छूटा है। इसीलिए, भविष्य मुझे आशा से पूर्ण दिखाई देता है।

तांडवी तेज फिर से हुंकार उठा है,
लोहित में था जो गिरा, कुठार उठा है।

कलकत्ता —**दिनकर**
9-1-1963 ई.

द्वितीय संस्करण की भूमिका

खुशी की बात है कि 'परशुराम की प्रतीक्षा' का द्वितीय संस्करण प्रकाशित हो रहा है। जनता ने इस कविता के प्रति जो प्रेम और उत्साह दिखाया है, वह इस बात का प्रमाण है कि हमारी जाति का समीपवर्ती भविष्य उज्ज्वल और महान् है।

प्रथम संस्करण में 'आज कसौटी पर गांधी की आग है' नामक कविता में एक पद छपने से छूट गया था। वह कमी इस बार पूरी की जा रही है।

भागलपुर —**दिनकर**
7-3-1965 ई.

क्रम

परशुराम की प्रतीक्षा

परशुराम की प्रतीक्षा

खण्ड : एक

गरदन पर किसका पाप वीर! ढोते हो?
शोणित से तुम किसका कलंक धोते हो?

उनका, जिनमें कारुण्य असीम तरल था,
तारुण्य-ताप था नहीं, न रंच गरल था;
सस्ती सुकीर्ति पाकर जो फूल गये थे,
निर्वीर्य कल्पनाओं में भूल गये थे;

गीता में जो त्रिपिटक-निकाय पढ़ते हैं,
तलवार गलाकर जो तकली गढ़ते हैं;
शीतल करते हैं अनल प्रबुद्ध प्रजा का,
शेरों को सिखलाते हैं धर्म अजा का;

सारी वसुन्धरा में गुरु-पद पाने को,
प्यासी धरती के लिए अमृत लाने को
जो सन्त लोग सीधे पाताल चले थे,
(अच्छे हैं अब : पहले भी बहुत भले थे।)

हम उसी धर्म की लाश यहाँ ढोते हैं,
शोणित से संतों का कलंक धोते हैं।

खण्ड : दो

हे वीर बन्धु! दायी है कौन विपद का?
हम दोषी किसको कहें तुम्हारे वध का?

यह गहन प्रश्न; कैसे रहस्य समझाएँ?
दस-बीस वधिक हों तो हम नाम गिनाएँ?
पर, कदम-कदम पर यहाँ खड़ा पातक है,
हर तरफ लगाये घात खड़ा घातक है।

घातक है, जो देवता-सदृश दिखता है,
लेकिन, कमरे में ग़लत हुक्म लिखता है।
जिस पापी को गुण नहीं; गोत्र प्यारा है,
समझो, उसने ही हमें यहाँ मारा है।

जो सत्य जान कर भी न सत्य कहता है,
या किसी लोभ के विवश मूक रहता है,
उस कुटिल राजतंत्री कदर्य को धिक् है,
यह मूक सत्यहन्ता कम नहीं वधिक है।

चोरों के हैं जो हितू, ठगों के बल हैं,
जिनके प्रताप से पलते पाप सकल हैं,
जो छल-प्रपंच, सब को प्रश्रय देते हैं,
या चाटुकार जन से सेवा लेते हैं;

यह पाप उन्हीं का हमको मार गया है,
भारत अपने घर में ही हार गया है।

है कौन यहाँ, कारण जो नहीं विपद् का?
किस पर ज़िम्मा है नहीं हमारे वध का?
जो चरम पाप है, हमें उसी की लत है,
दैहिक बल को कहता यह देश ग़लत है।

नेता निमग्न दिन-रात शान्ति-चिन्तन में,
कवि-कलाकार ऊपर उड़ रहे गगन में।
यज्ञाग्नि हिन्द में समिध नहीं पाती है,
पौरुष की ज्वाला रोज़ बुझी जाती है।

ओ बदनसीब अन्धो! कमज़ोर अभागो?
अब भी तो खोलो नयन, नींद से जागो।
वह अघी, बाहुबल का जो अपलापी है,
जिसकी ज्वाला बुझ गयी, वही पापी है।

जब तक प्रसन्न यह अनल, सुगुण हँसते हैं;
है जहाँ खड्ग, सब पुण्य वहीं बसते हैं।
वीरता जहाँ पर नहीं, पुण्य का क्षय है,
वीरता जहाँ पर नहीं, स्वार्थ की जय है।

तलवार पुण्य की सखी, धर्मपालक है,
लालच पर अंकुश कठिन, लोभ-सालक है।
असि छोड़ भीरु बन जहाँ धर्म सोता है,
पातक प्रचण्डतम वहीं प्रकट होता है।

तलवारें सोतीं जहाँ बन्द म्यानों में,
क़िस्मतें वहाँ सड़ती हैं तहखानों में।
बलिवेदी पर बालियाँ-नथें चढ़ती हैं,
सोने की ईंटें, मगर, नहीं कढ़ती हैं।

पूछो कुबेर से, कब सुवर्ण वे देंगे?
यदि आज नहीं तो सुयश और कब लेंगे?
तूफान उठेगा, प्रलय-बाण छूटेगा,
है जहाँ स्वर्ण, बम वहीं, स्यात्, फूटेगा।

जो करें, किन्तु, कंचन यह नहीं बचेगा,
शायद, सुवर्ण पर ही संहार मचेगा।
हम पर अपने पापों का बोझ न डालें,
कह दो सबसे, अपना दायित्व सँभालें।

कह दो प्रपंचकारी, कपटी, जाली से,
आलसी, अकर्मठ, काहिल, हड़ताली से,

सी लें ज़बान, चुपचाप काम पर जाएँ,
हम यहाँ रक्त, वे घर में स्वेद बहाएँ।

हम दें तुमको विजय, हमें तुम बल दो,
दो शस्त्र और अपना संकल्प अटल दो।
हों खड़े लोग कटिबद्ध वहाँ यदि घर में,
है कौन हमें जीते जो यहाँ समर में?

हो जहाँ कहीं भी अनय, उसे रोको रे!
जो करें पाप शशि-सूर्य, उन्हें टोको रे!

जा कहो, पुण्य यदि बढ़ा नहीं शासन में,
या आग सुलगती रही प्रजा के मन में;
तामस बढ़ता यदि गया ढकेल प्रभा को,
निर्बन्ध पन्थ यदि मिला नहीं प्रतिभा को,

रिपु नहीं, यही अन्याय हमें मारेगा,
अपने घर में ही फिर स्वदेश हारेगा।

खण्ड : तीन

किरिचों पर कोई नया स्वप्न ढोते हो?
किस नयी फसल के बीज वीर! बोते हो?

दुर्दान्त दस्यु को सेल हूलते हैं हम;
यम की दंष्ट्रा से खेल झूलते हैं हम।
वैसे तो कोई बात नहीं कहने को,
हम टूट रहे केवल स्वतन्त्र रहने को।

सामने देशमाता का भव्य चरण है,
जिह्वा पर जलता हुआ एक, बस प्रण है,
काटेंगे अरि का मुण्ड कि स्वयं कटेंगे,
पीछे, परन्तु, सीमा से नहीं हटेंगे।

फूटेंगी खर निर्झरी तप्त कुण्डों से,
भर जायेगा नगराज रुण्ड-मुण्डों से।
माँगेगी जो रणचण्डी भेंट, चढ़ेगी,
लाशों पर चढ़ कर आगे फ़ौज बढ़ेगी।

पहली आहुति है अभी, यज्ञ चलने दो,
दो हवा, देश की आग ज़रा जलने दो।
जब हृदय-हृदय पावक से भर जायेगा,
भारत का पूरा पाप उतर जायेगा;

देखोगे, कैसा प्रलय चण्ड़ होता है!
असिवन्त हिन्द कितना प्रचण्ड होता है!

बाँहों से हम अम्बुधि अगाध थाहेंगे,
धँस जायेगी यह धरा, अगर चाहेंगे।
तूफान हमारे इंगित पर ठहरेंगे,
हम जहाँ कहेंगे, मेघ वहीं घहरेंगे।

जो असुर, हमें सुर समझ, आज हँसते हैं,
वंचक श्रृंगाल भूँकते, साँप डँसते हैं,
कल यही कृपा के लिए हाथ जोड़ेंगे,
भृकुटी विलोक दुष्टता-द्वन्द्व छोड़ेंगे।

गरजो, अम्बर को भरो रणोच्चारों से,
क्रोधान्ध रोर, हाँकों से, हुंकारों से।
यह आग मात्र सीमा की नहीं लपट है,
मूढ़ो! स्वतन्त्रता पर ही यह संकट है।

जातीय गर्व पर क्रूर प्रहार हुआ है,
माँ के किरीट पर ही यह वार हुआ है।
अब जो सिर पर आ पड़े, नहीं डरना है,
जनमे हैं तो दो बार नहीं मरना है।

कुत्सित कलंक का बोध नहीं छोड़ेंगे,
हम बिना लिये प्रतिशोध नहीं छोड़ेंगे,
अरि का विरोध-अवरोध नहीं छोड़ेंगे,
जब तक जीवित हैं, क्रोध नहीं छोड़ेंगे।

गरजो हिमाद्रि के शिखर, तुंग पाटों पर,
गुलमर्ग, विन्ध्य, पश्चिमी, पूर्व घाटों पर,
भारत-समुद्र की लहर, ज्वार-भाटों पर,
गरजो, गरजो मीनार और लाटों पर।

खँडहरों, भग्न कोटों में, प्राचीरों में,
जाह्नवी, नर्मदा, यमुना के तीरों में,

कृष्णा-कछार में, कावेरी-कूलों में,
चित्तौड़-सिंहगढ़ के समीप धूलों में—

सोये हैं जो रणबली, उन्हें टेरो रे!
नूतन पर अपनी शिखा प्रत्न फेरो रे!

झकझोरो, झकझोरो महान् सुप्तों को,
टेरो, टेरो चाणक्य-चन्द्रगुप्तों को;
विक्रमी तेज, असि की उद्दाम प्रभा को,
राणा प्रताप, गोविन्द, शिवा, सरजा को;

वैराग्यवीर, बन्दा फकीर भाई को,
टेरो, टेरो माता लक्ष्मीबाई को।

आजन्म सहा जिसने न व्यंग्य थोड़ा था,
आजिज़ आ कर जिसने स्वदेश छोड़ा था,
हम हाय, आज तक जिसको गुहराते हैं,
'नेताजी अब आते हैं, अब आते हैं';

साहसी, शूर-रस के उस मतवाले को,
टेरो, टेरो आज़ाद हिन्दवाले को।

खोजो, टीपू सुलतान कहाँ सोये हैं?
अशफ़ाक़ और उसमान कहाँ सोये हैं?
बमवाले वीर जवान कहाँ सोये हैं?
वे भगतसिंह बलवान् कहाँ सोये हैं?

जा कहो, करें अब कृपा, नहीं रूठें वे,
बम उठा बाज़ के सदृश व्यग्र टूटें वे।

हम मान गये, जब क्रान्तिकाल होता है,
सारी लपटों का रंग लाल होता है।
जाग्रत पौरुष प्रज्वलित ज्वाला होना है,
शूरत्व नहीं कोमल, कराल होता है।

वास्तविक मर्म जीवन का जान गये हैं,
हम भली भाँति अघ को पहचान गये हैं।
हम समझ गये हैं खूब धर्म के छल को,
बम की महिमा को और विनय के बल को।

हम मान गये, वे धीर नहीं उद्धत थे,
वे सही, और हम विनयी बहुत ग़लत थे।
जा कहो, करें अब क्षमा, नहीं रूठें वे;
बम उठा बाज़ के सदृश व्यग्र टूटें वे।

साधना स्वयं शोणित कर धार रही है,
सतलज को साबरमती पुकार रही है।

वे उठें, देश उनके पीछे हो लेगा,
हम कहते हैं, कोई न व्यंग्य बोलेगा।
है कौन मूढ़, जो पिटक आज खोलेगा?
बोलेगा जय वह भी, न खड्ग जो लेगा।

वे उठें, हाय, नाहक विलम्ब होता है,
अपनी भूलों के लिए देश रोता है।

जिसका सारा इतिहास तप्त, जगमग है,
वीरता-वह्नि से भरी हुई रग-रग है,
जिसके इतने बेटे रण झेल चुके हैं,
शूली, किरीच, शोलों से खेल चुके हैं,

उस वीर जाति को बन्दी कौन करेगा?
विकराल आग मुट्ठी में कौन धरेगा?

केवल कृपाण को नहीं, त्याग-तप को भी,
टेरो, टेरो साधना, यज्ञ, जप को भी।
गरजो, तरंग से भरी आग भड़काओ,
हों जहाँ तपी, तप से तुम उन्हें जगाओ।

युग-युग से जो ऋद्धियाँ यहाँ उतरी हैं,
सिद्धियाँ धर्म की जो भी छिपी, धरी हैं,
उन सभी पावकों से प्रचण्डतम रण दो,
शर और शाप, दोनों को आमंत्रण दो।

चिन्तको! चिन्तना की तलवार गढ़ो रे!
ऋषियो! कृशानु-उद्दीपन मंत्र पढ़ो रे!
योगियो! जगो, जीवन की ओर बढ़ो रे!
बन्दूकों पर अपना आलोक मढ़ो रे!

है जहाँ कहीं भी तेज, हमें पाना है,
रण में समग्र भारत को ले जाना है।

पर्वतपति को आमूल डोलना होगा,
शंकर को ध्वंसक नयन खोलना होगा।
असि पर अशोक को मुण्ड तोलना होगा,
गौतम को जय जयकार बोलना होगा।

यह नहीं शान्ति की गुफा, युद्ध है, रण है,
तप नहीं, आज केवल तलवार शरण है।
ललकार रहा भारत को स्वयं मरण है,
हम जीतेंगे यह समर, हमारा प्रण है।

खण्ड : चार

कुछ पता नहीं, हम कौन बीज बोते हैं;
है कौन स्वप्न, हम जिसे यहाँ ढोते हैं।

पर, हाँ, वसुधा दानी है, नहीं कृपण है,
देता मनुष्य जब भी उसको जल-कण है;
यह दान वृथा वह कभी नहीं लेती है,
बदले में कोई दूब हमें देती है।

पर, हमने तो सींचा है उसे लहू से,
चढ़ती उमंग की कलियों की खुशबू से।
क्या यह अपूर्व बलिदान पचा वह लेगी?
उद्दाम राष्ट्र क्या हमें नहीं वह देगी?

ना, यह अकाण्ड दुष्काण्ड नहीं होने का,
यह जगा देश अब और नहीं सोने का।
जब तक भीतर की गाँस नहीं कढ़ती है,
श्री नहीं पुनः भारत-मुख पर चढ़ती है,

कैसे स्वदेश की रूह चैन पायेगी?
किस नर-नारी को भला नींद आयेगी?

कुछ सोच रहा है समय राह में थम कर,
है ठहर गया सहसा इतिहास सहम कर।
सदियों में शिव का अचल ध्यान डोला है,
तोपों के भीतर से भविष्य बोला है।

चोटें पड़ती यदि रहीं, शिला टूटेगी,
भारत में कोई नयी धार फूटेगी।

हम खड़े ध्वंस में जब भी कुछ गुनते हैं,
रथ के घर्घर का नाद कहीं सुनते हैं।
जिसकी आशा में खड़ा व्यग्र जन-जन है,
यह उसी वीर का, स्यात् वज्र-स्यन्दन है।

अम्बर में जो अप्रतिम क्रोध छाया है,
पावक जो हिम को फोड़ निकल आया है,
वह किसी भाँति भी वृथा नहीं जायेगा,
आयेगा, अपना महा वीर आयेगा।

हाँ, वही, रूप प्रज्वलित विभासित नर का,
अंशावतार सम्मिलित विष्णु-शंकर का।
हाँ, वही, दुरित से जो न सन्धि करता है,
जो संत धर्म के लिए खड्ग धरता है।

हाँ, वही फूटता जो समष्टि के मन से,
संचित करता है तेज व्यग्र जन-जन से।
हाँ, वही, न्याय-वंचित की जो आशा है,
निर्धनों, दीन-दलितों की अभिलाषा है।

विद्युत बनकर जो चमक रहा चिन्तन में,
गुंजित जिसका निर्घोष लोक-गर्जन में,
जो पतन-पुंज पर पावक बरसाता है,
यह उसी वीर का रथ दौड़ा आता है।

गाओ कवियो! जयगान, कल्पना तानो,
आ रहा देवता जो, उसको पहचानो।
है एक हाथ में परशु, एक में कुश है,
आ रहा नये भारत का भाग्यपुरुष है।

अंगार-हार अरपो, अर्चना करो रे!
आँखों की ज्वालाएँ मत देख डरो रे!
यह असुर भाव का शत्रु, पुण्य-त्राता है,
भयभीत मनुज के लिए अभय-दाता है।

यह वज्र वज्र के लिए, सुमों का सुम है;
यह और नहीं कोई, केवल हम-तुम हैं।

यह नहीं जाति का, न तो गोत्र-बन्धन का;
आ रहा मित्र भारत-भर के जन-जन का।

गांधी-गौतम का त्याग लिये आता है,
शंकर का शुद्ध विराग लिये आता है।
सच है, आँखों में आग लिये आता है,
पर, यह स्वदेश का भाग लिये आता है।

मत डरो, संत यह मुकुट नहीं माँगेगा,
धन के निमित्त यह धर्म नहीं त्यागेगा।
तुम सोओगे, तब भी यह ऋषि जागेगा,
ठन गया युद्ध तो बम-गोले दागेगा।

जब किसी जाति का अहं चोट खाता है,
पावक प्रचण्ड हो कर बाहर आता है।
यह वही चोट खाये स्वदेश का बल है,
आहत भुजंग है, सुलगा हुआ अनल है।

विक्रमी रूप नूतन अर्जुन-जेता का,
आ रहा स्वयं यह परशुराम त्रेता का।
यह उत्तेजित, साकार, क्रुद्ध भारत है,
यह और नहीं कोई, विशुद्ध भारत है।

पापों पर बनकर प्रलय-बाण छूटेगा,
यह क्लीव धर्म पर बाज़-सदृश टूटेगा।
जो रुष्ट खड्ग से हैं, उनसे रूठेगा,
कृत्रिम विभाकरों का प्रकाश लूटेगा।

वह गरुड़ देश का नाग-पाश काटेगा,
अरि-मुण्डों से खाइयाँ-खोह पाटेगा।
विद्युतित जीभ से चाट भीति हर लेगा,
वह तुम्हें आप अपने समान कर लेगा।

रह जायेगा वह नहीं ज्ञान सिखला कर,
दूरस्थ गगन में इन्द्रधनुष दिखला कर।
वह लक्ष्यविन्दु तक तुम को ले जायेगा,
उँगलियाँ थाम मंजिल तक पहुँचायेगा।

हर धड़कन पर वह सजल मेघ सिहरेगा,
गत और अनागत बीच व्यग्र बिहरेगा।
बरसेगा वन जलधार तृषित धानों पर,
बन तडिद्धार छूटेगा चट्टानों पर।

जब वह आयेगा, द्विधा-द्वन्द्व बिनसेगा,
आलिंगन में अवनी को व्योम कसेगा।
विज्ञान धर्म के धड़ से भिन्न न होगा,
भवितव्य भूत-गौरव से छिन्न न होगा

जब वह आयेगा, खल कुबुद्धि छोड़ेंगे,
सब साँप आप ही फण अपने तोड़ेंगे,
विषवाह-अभ्र गांधी पर नहीं घिरेंगे,
शान्ति के नीड़ में गोले नहीं गिरेंगे।

खण्ड : पाँच

[1]

सिखलायेगा वह, ऋत एक ही अनल है,
ज़िन्दगी नहीं वह, जहाँ नहीं हलचल है।
जिनमें दाहकता नहीं, न तो गर्जन है,
सुख की तरंग का जहाँ अन्ध वर्जन है,
जो सत्य राख में सने, रूक्ष, रूठे हैं,
छोड़ो उनको, वे सही नहीं, झूठे हैं।

[2]

वैराग्य छोड़ बाँहों की विभा सँभालो,
चट्टानों की छाती से दूध निकालो।
है रुकी जहाँ भी धार, शिलाएँ तोड़ो,
पीयूष चन्द्रमाओं को पकड़ निचोड़ो।
चढ़ तुंग शैल-शिखरों पर सोम पियो रे!
योगियों नहीं, विजयी के सदृश जियो रे!

[3]

मत टिको मदिर, मधुमयी, शान्त छाया में,
भूलो मत उज्जवल ध्येय मोह-माया में।
लौलुप्य-लालसा जहाँ, वहीं पर क्षय है;
आनन्द नहीं, जीवन का लक्ष्य विजय है।
जृम्भक, रहस्य-धूमिल मत ऋचा रचो रे!
सर्पित प्रसून के मद से बचो, बचो रे!

[4]

जब कुपित काल धीरता त्याग जलता है,
चिनगी बन फूलों का पराग जलता है,
सौन्दर्य-बोध बन नयी आग जलता है,
ऊँचा उठकर कामार्त राग जलता है।
अम्बर पर अपनी विभा प्रबुद्ध करो रे!
गरजे कृशानु, तब कंचन शुद्ध करो रे!

[5]

भामा ह्लादिनी-तरंग, तडिन्माला है,
वह नहीं काम की लता, वीर बाला है,
आधी हालाहल-धार, अर्ध ज्वाला है।
जब भी उठती हुंकार युद्ध-ज्वाला है,
चण्डिका कान्त को मुण्ड-माल देती है;
रथ के चक्के में भुजा डाल देती है।

[6]

खोजता पुरुष सौन्दर्य, त्रिया प्रतिभा को,
नारी चरित्र-बल को, नर मात्र त्वचा को।
श्री नहीं पाणि जिसके सिर पर धरती है,
भामिनी हृदय से उसे नहीं वरती है।
पाओ रमणी का हृदय विजय अपनाकर,
या बसो वहाँ बन कसक वीर-गति पाकर।

[7]

जिसकी बाँहें बलमयी, ललाट अरुण है,
भामिनी वही तरुणी, नर वही तरुण है।
है वही प्रेम जिसकी तरंग उच्छल है,
वारुणी-धार में मिश्रित जहाँ गरल है।
उद्दाम प्रीति बलिदान-बीज बोती है;
तलवार प्रेम से और तेज़ होती है।

[8]

पी जिसे उमड़ता अनल, भुजा भरती है,
वह शक्ति सूर्य की किरणों में झरती है।
मरु के प्रदाह में छिपा हुआ जो रस है,
तूफान-अन्धड़ों में जो अमृत-कलस है,
उस तपन-तत्त्व से हृदय-प्राण सींचो रे!
खींचो, भीतर आँधियाँ और खींचो रे!

[9]

छोड़ो मत अपनी आन, सीस कट जाये,
मत झुको अनय पर, भले व्योम फट जाये।
दो बार नहीं यमराज कण्ठ धरता है,
मरता है जो, एक ही बार मरता है।
तुम स्वयं मरण के मुख पर चरण धरो रे!
जीना हो तो मरने से नहीं डरो रे!

[10]

स्वातन्त्र्य जाति की लगन, व्यक्ति की धुन है,
बाहरी वस्तु यह नहीं, भीतरी गुण है।
नत हुए बिना जो अशनि-घात सहती है,
स्वाधीन जगत् में वही जाति रहती है।
वीरत्व छोड़ पर का मत चरण गहो रे!
जो पड़े आन, खुद ही सब आग सहो रे!

[11]

दासत्व जहाँ है, वहीं स्तब्ध जीवन है,
स्वातन्त्र्य निरन्तर समर, सनातन रण है।
स्वातन्त्र्य समस्या नहीं आज या कल की,
जागृति तीव्र वह घड़ी-घड़ी, पल-पल की।
पहरे पर चारों ओर स्तर्क लगो रे!
धर धनुष-बाण उद्यत दिन-रात जगो रे!

[12]

आँधियाँ नहीं जिसमें उमंग भरती हैं,
छातियाँ जहाँ संगीनों से डरती हैं,
शोणित के बदले जहाँ अश्रु बहता है,
वह देश कभी स्वाधीन नहीं रहता है।
पकड़ो अयाल, अन्धड़ पर उछल चढ़ो रे!
किरिचों पर अपने तन का चाम मढ़ो रे!

[13]

जब कभी अहं पर नियति चोट देती है,
कुछ चीज़ अहं से बड़ी जन्म लेती है।
नर पर जब भी भीषण विपत्ति आती है,
वह उसे और दुर्धर्ष बना जाती है।
चोटें खाकर बिफरो, कुछ अधिक तनो रे!
धधको, स्फुलिंग-से, बढ़ अंगार बनो रे!

[14]

धन-धाम, ज्ञान-विज्ञान मात्र सम्बल है,
बस, एक मात्र बलिदान जाति का बल है।
सिर देने में जो लोग नहीं डरते हैं,
वे ही प्रभंजनों पर शासन करते हैं।
जब पड़े विपद्, अपनी उमंग जाँचो रे!
विकराल काल के फण पर चढ़ नाचो रे!

[15]

हैं खड़े हिंस्र वृक-व्याघ्र, खड़ा पशुबल है;
ऊँची मनुष्यता का पथ नहीं सरल है।
ये हिंस्र साधु पर भी न तरस खाते हैं,
कण्ठी-माला के सहित चबा जाते हैं।
जो वीर काट कर इन्हें पार जायेगा,
उत्तुंग शृंग पर वही पहुँच पायेगा।

[16]

जो पुरुष भूल शायक, कुठार को, असि को,
पूजता मात्र चिन्तन, विचार को, मसि को,
सत्य का नहीं बहुमान किया करता है,
केवल सपनों का ध्यान किया करता है,
बस में उसके यह लोक न रह जायेगा।
है हवा स्वप्न, कर में वह क्यों आयेगा?

[17]

उपशम को ही जो जाति धर्म कहती है,
शम, दम, विराग को श्रेष्ठ कर्म कहती है,
धृति को प्रहार, क्षान्ति को वर्म कहती है,
अक्रोध, विनय को विजय-मर्म कहती है,
अपमान कौन, वह जिसको नहीं सहेगी?
सब को असीस, सब का बन दास रहेगी।

[18]

यह कठिन शाप सुकुमार धर्म-साधन का,
रण-विमुख, शान्त जीवन के आराधन का;
जातियाँ पावकों से बचकर चलती हैं।
निर्वीर्य कल्पनाएँ रच कर चलती हैं।
वृन्तों पर जलते सूर्य छोड़ देती हैं,
चुन-चुन कर केवल चाँद तोड़ लेती हैं।

[19]

दो उन्हें राम, तो मात्र नाम वे लेंगी,
विक्रमी शरासन से न काम वे लेंगी;
नवनीत बना देतीं भट अवतारी को,
मोहन मुरलीधर पांचजन्य-धारी को।
पावक को बुझा तुषार बना देती हैं,
गांधी को शीतल क्षार बना देती हैं।

[20]

है सही, बना पहले पृथ्वी से जल था,
पर, बहुत पूर्व उससे बन चुका अनल था।
जब प्रथम-प्रथम हो उठा तत्त्व चंचल था,
प्रेरणा-स्रोत पर विनय नहीं थी, बल था।
है अनल ब्रह्म, पावक-तरंग जीवन है,
अब समझा, क्यों ज्वाला अभंग जीवन है?

[21]

भव को न अग्नि करने को क्षार बनी थी,
रखने को, बस, उज्ज्वल आचार बनी थी।
शिव नहीं, शक्ति सर्जन-आधार बनी थी;
जब बनी सृष्टि, पहले तलवार बनी थी।
वह कालकण्ठ स्रज नहीं, न कुंकुम-रज है।
सत्य ही कहा गुरु ने, अकाल असि-ध्वज है।

[22]

स्वर में पावक यदि नहीं, वृथा वन्दन है,
वीरता नहीं, तो सभी विनय क्रन्दन है।
सिर पर जिसके असिघात, रक्त-चन्दन है,
भ्रामरी उसी का करती अभिनन्दन है।
दानवी रक्त से सभी पाप धुलते हैं,
ऊँची मनुष्यता के पथ भी खुलते हैं।

[23]

सत्य है, धर्म का परम रूप यव-कुश है,
अत्यय-अधर्म पर परशु मात्र अंकुश है,
पर, जब कुठार की धार क्षीण होती है,
स्वयमेव दर्भ की श्री मलीन होती है।
हो धर्म ध्येय, तो भजो प्रथम बाँहों को।
तोलो अपना बल-वीर्य, नहीं आहों को।

[24]

हैं दुखी मेष, क्यों लहू शेर चखते हैं,
नाहक इतने क्यों दाँत तेज़ रखते हैं।
पर, शेर द्रवित हो दशन तोड़ क्यों लेंगे?
मेषों के हित व्याघ्रता छोड़ क्यों देंगे?
एक ही पन्थ, तुम भी आघात हनो रे!
मेषत्व छोड़ मेषो! तुम व्याघ्र बनो रे!

[25]

जो अड़े, शेर उस नर से डर जाता है,
है विदित, व्याघ्र को व्याघ्र नहीं खाता है।
सच पूछो तो अब भी सच यही वचन है,
सभ्यता क्षीण, बलवान हिंस्र कानन है।
एक ही पन्थ अब भी जग में जीने का,
अभ्यास करो छागियो! रक्त पीने का।

[26]

जब शान्तिवादियों ने कपोत छोड़े थे,
किसने आशा से नहीं हाथ जोड़े थे?
पर, हाय, धर्म यह भी धोखा है, छल है;
उजले कबूतरों में भी छिपा अनल है।
पंजों में इनके धार धरी होती है,
कइयों में तो बारूद भरी होती है।

[27]

जो पुण्य-पुण्य बक रहे, उन्हें बकने दो,
जैसे सदियाँ थक चुकीं, उन्हें थकने दो।
पर, देख चुके हम तो सब पुण्य कमा कर,
सौभाग्य, मान, गौरव, अभिमान गँवा कर।
वे पियें शीत, तुम आतप-घाम पियो रे!
वे जपें नाम, तुम बन कर राम जियो रे!

[28]

हैं जिन्हें दाँत, उनसे अदन्त कहते हैं,
यानी शूरों को देख सन्त कहने हैं,
"तुम तुड़ा दाँत क्यों नहीं पुण्य पाने हो?
यानी तुम भी क्यों भेड़ न बन जाते हो?"
पर कौन शेर भेड़ों की बात सुनेगा,
ज़िन्दगी छोड़ मरने की राह चुनेगा?

[29]

सुर नहीं शान्ति आँसू बिखेर लायेंगे;
मृग नहीं, युद्ध का शमन शेर लायेंगे।
विनयी न विनय को लगा टेर लायेंगे,
लायेंगे तो वह दिन दिलेर लायेंगे।
बोलती बन्द होगी पशु की जब भय से,
उतरेगी भू पर शान्ति छूट संशय से।

[30]

वे देश शान्ति के सब से शत्रु प्रबल हैं,
जो बहुत बड़े होने पर भी दुर्बल हैं,
है जिनके उदर विशाल, बाँह छोटी है,
भोथरे दाँत, पर, जीभ बहुत मोटी है।
औरों के पाले जो अलज्ज पलते हैं,
अथवा शेरों पर लदे हुए चलते हैं।

[31]

सिंहों पर अपना अतुल भार मत डालो,
हाथियो! स्वयं अपना तुम बोझ सँभालो।
यदि लदे फिरे, यों ही, तो पछताओगे,
शव मात्र आप अपना तुम रह जाओगे।
यह नहीं मात्र अपकीर्ति, अनय की अति है।
जाने, कैसे सहती यह दृश्य प्रकृति है!

[32]

उद्देश्य जन्म का नहीं कीर्ति या धन है,
सुख नहीं, धर्म भी नहीं, न तो दर्शन है;
विज्ञान, ज्ञान-बल नहीं, न तो चिन्तन है,
जीवन का अन्तिम ध्येय स्वयं जीवन है।
सबसे स्वतन्त्र यह रस जो अनघ पियेगा,
पूरा जीवन केवल वह वीर जियेगा।

[33]

जीवन गति है, वह नित अरुद्ध चलता है,
पहला प्रमाण पावक का, वह जलता है।
सिखला निरोध-निर्ज्वलन धर्म छलता है,
जीवन तरंग-गर्जन है, चंचलता है।
धधको अभंग, पल-विपल अरुद्ध जलो रे!
धारा रोके यदि राह, विरुद्ध चलो रे!

[34]

जीवन अपनी ज्वाला से आप ज्वलित है,
अपनी तरंग से आप समुद्वेलित है।
तुम वृथा ज्योति के लिए कहाँ जाओगे?
है जहाँ आग, आलोक वहीं पाओगे।
क्या हुआ, पत्र यदि मृदुल, सुरम्य कली है?
सब मृषा, तना तरु का यदि नहीं बली है।

[35]

धन से मनुष्य का पाप उभर आता है,
निर्धन जीवन यदि हुआ, बिखर जाता है।
कहते हैं जिसको सुयश-कीर्ति, सो क्या है?
कानों की यदि गुदगुदी नहीं, तो क्या है?
यश-अयश-चिन्तना भूल स्थान पकड़ो रे!
यश नहीं, मात्र जीवन के लिए लड़ो रे!

[36]

कुछ समझ नहीं पड़ता, रहस्य यह क्या है!
जाने, भारत में बहती कौन हवा है!
गमलों में हैं जो खड़े, सुरम्य-सुदल हैं,
मिट्टी पर के ही पेड़ दीन-दुर्बल हैं।
जब तक है यह वैषम्य समाज सड़ेगा,
किस तरह एक होकर यह देश लड़ेगा।

[37]

सबसे पहले यह दुरित-मूल काटो रे!
समतल पीटो, खाइयाँ-खड्ग पाटो रे!
बहुपाद वटों की शिरा-सोर छाँटो रे!
जो मिले अमृत, सबको समान बाँटो रे!
वैषम्य घोर जब तक यह शेष रहेगा,
दुर्बल का ही दुर्बल यह देश रहेगा।

[38]

यह बड़े भाग्य की बात! सिन्धु चंचल है,
मथ रहा आज फिर उसे मंदराचल है।
छोड़ता व्यग्र फूत्कार सर्प पल-पल है,
गर्जित तरंग, प्रज्वलित वाडवानल है।
लो कढ़ा ज़हर! संसार जला जाता है।
ठहरो, ठहरो, पीयूष अभी आता है।

[39]

पर, सावधान! जा कहो उन्हें समझा कर,
सुर पुनः भाग जायें मत सुधा चुरा कर।
जो कढ़ा अमृत, सम-अंश बाँट हम लेंगे,
इस बार ज़हर का भाग उन्हें भी देंगे।
वैषम्य शेष यदि रहा, क्षान्ति डोलेगी,
इस रण पर चढ़ कर महा क्रान्ति बोलेगी।

[40]

झंझा-झकोर पर चढ़ो, मस्त झूलो रे!
वृन्तों पर बन पावक-प्रसून फूलो रे!
दायें-बायें का द्वन्द्व आज भूलो रे!
सामने पड़े जो शत्रु, शूल हूलो रे!
वृक हो कि व्याल, जो भी विरुद्ध आयेगा,
भारत से जीवित लौट नहीं पायेगा।

[41]

निर्जर पिनाक हर का टंकार उठा है,
हिमवन्त हाथ में ले अंगार उठा है,
ताण्डवी तेज फिर से हुंकार उठा है,
लोहित में था जो गिरा, कुठार उठा है।
संसार धर्म की नई आग देखेगा,
मानव का करतब पुनः नाग देखेगा।

[42]

माँगो, माँगो वरदान धाम चारों से,
मन्दिरों, मस्जिदों, गिरजों, गुरुद्वारों से।
जय कहो वीर विक्रम की, शिवा बली की,
उस धर्मखड्ग, ईश्वर के सिंह, अली की।
जब मिले काल, जय महाकाल!' बोलो रे!
सत् श्री अकाल! सत श्री अकाल! बोलो रे!

[7-1-1963]

जवानियाँ

नये सुरों में शिंजिनी बजा रहीं जवानियाँ,
लहू में तैर-तैर के नहा रहीं जवानियाँ।

[1]

प्रभात-शृंग से घड़े सुवर्ण के उँड़ेलती,
रँगी हुई घटा में भानु को उछाल खेलती;
तुषार-जाल में सहस्र हेम-दीप बालती,
समुद्र की तरंग में हिरण्य-धूलि डालती;
सुनील चीर को सुवर्ण-बीच बोरती हुई,
धरा के ताल-ताल में उसे निचोड़ती हुई;
उषा के हाथ की विभा लुटा रहीं जवानियाँ।

[2]

घनों के पार बैठ तार बीन के चढ़ा रहीं,
सुमन्द्र नाद में मलार विश्व को सुना रहीं;
अभी कढ़ी लटें निचोड़तीं, ज़मीन सींचतीं,
अभी बढ़ीं घटा में क्रुद्ध काल-खड्ग खींचतीं,

पड़ी व' टूट देख लो, अजस्र वारिधार में,
चलीं व' बाढ़ बन, नहीं समा सकीं कगार में।
रुकावटों को तोड़-फोड़ छा रहीं जवानियाँ।

[3]

हटो तमीचरो, कि हो चुकी समाप्त रात है,
कुहेलिका के पार जगमगा रहा प्रभात है।
लपेट में समेटता रुकावटों को तोड़ के,
प्रकाश का प्रवाह आ रहा दिगन्त फोड़ के!
विशीर्ण डालियाँ महीरुहों की टूटने लगीं;
शमा की झालरें व' टक्करों से फूटने लगीं।
चढ़ी हुई प्रभंजनों प' आ रहीं जवानियाँ।

[4]

घटा को फाड़ व्योम-बीच गूँजती दहाड़ है,
ज़मीन डोलती है और डोलता पहाड़ है;
भुजंग दिग्गजों से, कूर्मराज त्रस्त कोल से,
धरा उछल-उछल के बात पूछती खगोल से;
कि क्या हुआ है सृष्टि को? न एक अंग शान्त है;
प्रकोप रुद्र का कि कल्पनाश है, युगान्त है?
जवानियों की धूम-सी मचा रहीं जवानियाँ।

[5]

समस्त सूर्य-लोक एक हाथ में लिये हुए,
दबा के एक पाँव चन्द्र-भाल पर दिये हुए,
खगोल में धुआँ बिखेरती प्रतप्त श्वास से,
भविष्य को पुकारती हुई प्रचण्ड हास से;

उछाल देव-लोक को मही से तोलती हुईं,
मनुष्य के प्रताप का रहस्य खोलती हुईं;
विराट् रूप विश्व को दिखा रहीं जवानियाँ।

[6]

मही प्रदीप्त है, दिशा-दिगन्त लाल-लाल है,
व' देख लो, जवानियों की जल रही मशाल है;
व' गिर रहे हैं आग में पहाड़ टूट-टूट के,
व' आसमाँ से आ रहे हैं रत्न छूट-छूट के;
उठो, उठो कुरीतियों की राह तुम भी रोक दो,
बढ़ो, बढ़ो, कि आग में गुलामियों को झोंक दो।
परम्परा की होलिका जला रहीं जवानियाँ।

[7]

व' देख लो, खड़ी है कौन तोप के निशान पर;
व' देख लो, अड़ी है कौन ज़िन्दगी की आन पर।
व' कौन थी जो कूद के अभी गिरी है आग में?
लहू बहा? कि तेल आ गिरा नया चिराग में?
अहा 'व' अश्रु था कि प्रेम का दबा उफान था?
हँसी थी या कि चित्र में सजीव, मौन गान था?
अलभ्य भेंट काल को चढ़ा रहीं जवानियाँ।

[8]

अहा, कि एक रात चाँदनी-भरी सुहावनी,
अहा, कि एक बात प्रेम की बड़ी लुभावनी;

अहा, कि एक याद दूब-सी मरुप्रदेश में,
अहा, कि एक चाँद जो छिपा कराल वेश में;
अहा, पुकार कर्म की, अहा रे पीर मर्म की,
अहा, कि प्रीति भेंट जा चढ़ी कठोर धर्म की।
अहा, कि आँसुओं में मुस्कुरा रहीं जवानियाँ।

[1945 ई.]

हिम्मत की रौशनी

उसे भी देख, जो भीतर भरा अंगार है साथी!

[1]

सियाही देखता है, देखता है तू अँधेरे को,
किरण को घेर कर छाये हुए विकराल घेरे को।
उसे भी देख, जो इस बाहरी तम को बहा सकती,
दबी तेरे लहू में रौशनी की धार है साथी!

[2]

पड़ी थी नींव तेरी चाँद-सूरज के उजाले पर,
तपस्या पर, लहू पर, आग पर, तलवार-भाले पर।
डरे तू नाउम्मीदी से, कभी यह हो नहीं सकता,
कि तुझमें ज्योति का अक्षय भरा भण्डार है साथी!

[3]

बवण्डर चीखता लौटा, फिरा तूफ़ान जाता है,
डराने के लिए तुझको नया भूडोल आता है;
नया मैदान है राही, गरजना है नये बल से;
उठा इस बार वह जो आखिरी हुंकार है साथी!

[4]

विनय की रागिनी में बीन के ये तार बजते हैं,
रुदन बजता, सजग हो क्षोभ-हाहाकार बजते हैं।
बजा, इस बार दीपक-राग कोई आख़िरी सुर में;
छिपा इस बीन में ही आगवाला तार है साथी!

[5]

गरजते शेर आये, सामने फिर भेड़िये आये,
नखों को तेज़, दाँतों को बहुत तीखा किये आये।
मगर, परवाह क्या? हो जा खड़ा तू तानकर उसको,
छिपी जो हड्डियों में आग-सी तलवार है साथी!

[6]

शिखर पर तू, न तेरी राह बाकी दाहिने-बायें,
खड़ी आगे दरी यह मौत-सी विकराल मुँह बाये,
क़दम पीछे हटाया तो अभी ईमान जाता है,
उछल जा, कूद जा, पल में दरी यह पार है साथी?

[7]

न रुकना है तुझे झण्डा उड़ा केवल पहाड़ों पर,
विजय पानी है तुझको चाँद-सूरज पर, सितारों पर।
वधू रहती जहाँ नरवीर की, तलवारवालों की,
ज़मीं वह इस ज़रा से आसमाँ के पार है साथी।

[8]

भुजाओं पर मही का भार फूलों-सा उठाये जा,
कँपाये जा गगन को, इन्द्र का आसन हिलाये जा।
जहाँ में एक ही है रौशनी, वह नाम की तेरे,
ज़मीं को एक तेरी आग का आधार है साथी!

[1946 ई.]

लोहे के मर्द

पुरुष वीर बलवान,
देश की शान,
हमारे नौजवान
घायल होकर आये हैं।

कहते हैं, ये पुष्प, दीप
अक्षत क्यों लाये हो?

हमें कामना नहीं सुयश-विस्तार की,
फूलों के हारों की, जय-जयकार की।

तड़प रही घायल स्वदेश की शान है।
सीमा पर संकट में हिन्दुस्तान है।

ले जाओ आरती, पुष्प, पल्लव हरे,
ले जाओ ये थाल मोदकों से भरे।

तिलक चढ़ा मत और हृदय में हूक दो,
दे सकते हो तो गोली-बन्दूक़ दो।

[1962 ई.]

जनता जगी हुई है

जनता जगी हुई है।
क्रुद्ध सिंहिनी कुछ इस चिन्ता से भी ठगी हुई है।
कहाँ गये वे, जो पानी में आग लगाते थे?
बजा-बजा दुन्दुभी रात-दिन हमें जगाते थे?
धरती पर है कौन? कौन है सपनों के डेरों में?
कौन मुक्त? है घिरा कौन प्रस्तावों के घेरों में?
सोच न कर चण्डिके! भ्रमित हैं जो, वे भी आयेंगे।
तेरी छाया छोड़ अभागे शरण कहाँ पायेंगे?

जनता जगी हुई है।
भरत-भूमि में किसी पुण्य-पावक ने किया प्रवेश।
धधक उठा है एक दीप की लौ-सा सारा देश।
खौल रहीं नदियाँ, मेघों में शम्पा लहक रही है।
फट पड़ने को विकल शैल की छाती दहक रही है।
गर्जन, गूँज, तरंग, रोष, निर्घोष, हाँक हुंकार!
जाने, होगा शमित आज क्या खाकर पारावार!

जनता जगी हुई है।
ओ गांधी के शान्ति-सदन में आग लगानेवाले!
कपटी, कुटिल, कृतघ्न, आसुरी महिमा के मतवाले!
वैसे तो, मन मार शील से हम विनम्र जीते हैं,
आततायियों का शोणित, लेकिन, हम भी पीते हैं,
मुख में वेद, पीठ पर तरकस, कर में कठिन कुठा,
सावधान! ले रहा परशुधर फिर नवीन अवतार!

जनता जगी हुई है।
मूँद-मूँद वे पृष्ठ, शील का गुण जो सिखलाते हैं,
वज्रायुध को पाप, लौह को दुर्गुण बतलाते हैं।
मन की व्यथा समेट, न तो अपनेपन से हारेगा।
मर जायेगा स्वयं, सर्प को अगर नहीं मारेगा।
पर्वत पर से उतर रहा है महा भयानक व्याल।
मधुसूदन को टेर, नहीं यह सुगत बुद्ध का काल।

जनता जगी हुई है।
नाचे रणचण्डिका कि उतरे प्रलय हिमालय पर से,
फटे अतल पाताल कि झर-झर झरे मृत्यु अम्बर से;
झेल कलेजे पर, क़िस्मत की जो भी नाराज़ी है,
खेल मरण का खेल, मुक्ति की यह पहली बाज़ी है।
सिर पर उठा वज्र, आँखों पर ले हरि का अभिशाप।
अग्नि-स्नान के बिना धुलेगा नहीं राष्ट्र का पाप।

3-11-62 ई.]

आज कसौटी पर गांधी की आग है

[1]

अब भी पशु मत बनो,
कहा है वीर जवाहरलाल ने।

अन्धकार की दबी रौशनी की धीमी ललकार;
कठिन घड़ी में भी भारत के मन की धीर पुकार।
सुनती हो नागिनी! समझती हो इस स्वर को?
देखा है क्या कहीं और भू पर उस नर को—
जिसे न चढ़ता ज़हर,
न तो उन्माद कभी आता है;
समर-भूमि में भी जो
पशु होने से घबराता है?

[2]

अब भी पशु मत बनो,
कहा है वीर जवाहरलाल ने।

ऊँचाई की बात, किन्तु, कुछ चिन्ता भी है।
क्या मनुष्य मानव होकर लड़ने जाता है?
क्रूर दानवों के दुर्दान्त समूह ने,
वृकों, हिंस्र पशुओं, बाघों के व्यूह ने—
घेर लिया है जिसे, अगर वह नर पशुओं पर,
तुलसी की कण्ठी छू-छू, रो-रोकर वार करेगा,
पशु की होगी विजय, पराजय मानवता की
और, अन्त में, द्विधाग्रस्त मानव भी स्वयं मरेगा।

[3]

अब भी पशु मत बनो,
कहा है वीर जवाहरलाल ने।

पर, यह सुधा-तरंग कौन पीने देता है?
बिना हुए पशु आज कौन जीने देता है?

शुरू हो गया भैंस-भैंस का खेल,
जानवर तू भी बन ले;
पशु की तरह डकार,
यही वन की भाषा है।
सिर पर तीखे सींग बाँध,
बघनखे पहन ले।

सकुच रहा? क्या बर्बरता का खेल
नहीं खुलकर खेलेगा?
तोड़ेगा सिर नहीं विकट,
विषधर भुजंग का?

भैंसों की हुरपेट
पीठ पर ही झेलेगा?
तो कहता हूँ, सुन रहस्य की बात,
खड्ग सींचा जाता है—
नहीं युद्ध में गंगा के
जल की फुहार से।
अजब बात तू लड़े
आततायी असुरों से
निर्ममता से नहीं,
दया, ममता, दुलार से!

दबा पुण्य का वेग,
अँखड़ियाँ गीली मत होने दे;
कसकर पकड़ कृपाण,
मुट्ठियाँ ढीली मत होने दे।

जहाँ शस्त्रबल नहीं,
शास्त्र पछताते या रोते हैं।
ऋषियों को भी सिद्धि
तभी तप से मिलती है,
जब पहरे पर स्वयं
धनुर्धर राम खड़े होते हैं।

पापी कोई और, चित्त क्यों म्लान करें हम?
भारत में जो निधि मनुष्यता की संचित है,
क्यों पशुत्व-भय से उसका बलिदान करें हम?

किसे लीलने को आई यह लाल लपट है?
गांधी पर यदि नहीं, और किस पर संकट है?

सकुच गए यदि हम अहिंस्र
हिंसा के हाहाकार से,
कौन बचा पाएगा
गांधी को पशुओं की मार से?

समय पूछता है, ज्वाला है कहाँ अभय की?
कहाँ सत्य का वज्र, लौहमय रीढ़ विनय की?

कहाँ सिन्धु का अनल,
अधर पर जिसके इतना झाग है?
आज अहिंसा नहीं,
कसौटी पर गांधी की आग है।

[1962 ई.]

जौहर

जगता तभी जहान,
उसे जब विपद् जगाती है।

हँसी भूल बच्चे चिन्तन करने लगते हैं।
बहनें जातीं डूब किसी गम्भीर ध्यान में।
कुसुम खोजने लगते अपनी आग,
ऊँघती नदी तेज़ होकर हहराती है।

पेड़ खड़े कर कान प्रलय की चरण-चाप सुनते हैं,
हवा आँकने को भविष्य की आहट रुक जाती है,
आर-पार अम्बर के जब शम्पा चिल्लाती है।

भारत में जब कभी कड़कता वज्र,
सती भामिनियाँ सहसा हो उठतीं निर्मम, कठोर।
दाँतों से अधर दबा,
आँखों का अश्रु रोक,

बलि-बेला की आरती, पुष्प, रोली सहेज,
पुरुषों को रण में भेज
चण्डिकाएँ सगर्व
सिन्दूर लेप घर-घर उमँग शिखा सजाती हैं।

विजयी अगर स्वदेश,
प्रिया-प्रियतम का फिर नाता है।
विजयी अगर स्वदेश,
पुरुष फिर पुत्र, त्रिया माता है।

किन्तु, पताका झुकी अगर बलिदान की,
गरदन ऊँची रही न हिन्दुस्तान की,
पुरुष पीठ पर लिये घाव रोते रहें,
आँसू से अपना कलंक धोते रहें।

पर, जातीय कलंक
देश की माताएँ सहतीं नहीं;
परम्परा है, चीख़-चीख़
वे पीड़ाएँ कहतीं नहीं।

हारे नर को देख
देवियाँ दबी ग्लानि के भार से
जल उठती हैं, अगर
काट सकतीं न कष्ट तलवार से।

[1962 ई.]

आपद्धर्म

अरे उर्वशीकार!
कविता की गरदन पर धर कर पाँव खड़ा हो।
हमें चाहिए गर्म गीत, उन्माद प्रलय का,
अपनी ऊँचाई से तू कुछ और बड़ा हो।

कच्चा पानी ठीक नहीं,
ज्वर-ग्रसित देश है।
उबला हुआ समुष्ण सलिल है पथ्य,
वही परिशोधित जल दे।
जाड़े की है रात, गीत की गरमाहट दे,
तप्त अनल दे।
रोज़ पत्र आते हैं, जलते गान लिखूँ मैं,
जितना हूँ, उससे कुछ अधिक जवान दिखूँ मैं।

और, सत्य ही, मैं भी युग के ज्वरावेग से चूर,
दूर उर्वशी-लोक से,

गयी जवानी की बुझती भट्ठी फिर सुलगाता हूँ।
जितनी ही फैलती देश में भीति युद्ध की,
मैं उतना ही कण्ठ फाड़, कुछ और ज़ोर से,
चिल्लाता, चीख़ता, युद्ध के अन्ध गीत गाता हूँ।
किन्तु, हृदय से जब भी कोई आग उमड़ कर
चट्टानों की वज्र-मधुर रागिनी
कण्ठ-स्वर में भरने आती है,
ताप और आलोक, जहाँ दोनों बसते आये थे,
वहाँ दहकते अंगारे केवल धरने आती है;
तभी प्राण के किसी निभृत कोने से
कहता है कोई, माना, विस्फोट नहीं यह व्यर्थ है,
किन्तु, बुलाने को जिसको तू गरज रहा है,
उसे पास लाने में केवल गर्जन नहीं समर्थ है।

रोष, घोष, स्वर नहीं, मौन शूरता मनुज का धन है।
और शूरता नहीं मात्र अंगार,
शूरता नहीं मात्र रण में प्रकोप से धुँधुआती तलवार;
शूरता स्वस्थ जाति का चिर-अनिद्र, जाग्रत स्वभाव,
शूरत्व मृत्यु के वरने का निर्भीक भाव;
शूरत्व त्याग; शूरता बुद्धि की प्रखर आग;
शूरत्व मनुज का द्विधा-मुक्त चिन्तन है।

विजय-केतु गाड़ते वीर जिस गगनजयी चोटी पर,
पहले वह मन की उमंग के बीच चढ़ी जाती है,
विद्युत् बन छूटती समर में जो कृपाण लोहे की,
भट्ठी में पीछे, विचार में प्रथम गढ़ी जाती है।

आँख खोलकर देख, बड़ी से बड़ी सिद्धि का
कारण केवल एक अंग तलवार है;
तीन अंश उसका निमित्त संकल्प-शुद्धि है,
आशा है, साहस है, शुद्ध विचार है।

सोच, कहाँ है उस दुरन्त,
पापिनी बुद्धि का मूल, तुझे जो
बार-बार आकर अपनी छलना से छल जाती है?
बार-बार तू उदय-शृंग पर चढ़ क्यों गिर जाता है?
बार-बार कर में आकर क्यों सिद्धि निकल जाती है?
ओ विराग को सकल सुकृत का मर्म समझनेवाले!
आत्मघात को उच्च धर्म के हित अर्पित बलिदान,
शत्रु के रक्त-पान को
मानवता का पतन, कलुष का कर्म समझनेवाले!

ओ निरग्नि! ओ शान्त! प्रश्न तेरा गम्भीर, गहन है।
रोष, घोष, हुंकार, गर्जनों से उद्धार न होगा।
भुजा नहीं बलहीन,
रक्त की आभा नहीं मलीन,
अरे, ओ नर पवित्र! प्राचीन!
दीन, लेकिन, तेरा चिन्तन है।

विजय चाहता है, सचमुच,
तू अगर विषैले नाग पर,
तो कहता हूँ, सुन,
दिल में जो आग लगी है,
उसे बुद्धि में घोल,
उठाकर ले जा उसे दिमाग़ पर।

तुझसे जो माँगते उबलते गीत अनल के,
पूछ कि वे कूटस्थ आग लेकर क्या भला करेंगे?
क्या प्रमाण है, यह सूखी बारूद नहीं सीलेगी?
घर में बिखरी हुई बर्फ वे कहाँ समेट धरेंगे?

अच्छा है, वे लड़ें नहीं, जिनके जीवन में
विचिकित्सा जीवित है धर्म-अधर्म की।
अच्छा है, वे अड़ें आन पर नहीं,
न खेलें कभी जान पर,
चबा रही है जिन्हें युगों से
दुविधा कर्म-अकर्म की।
क्योंकि युद्ध में जीत कभी भी उसे नहीं मिलती है,
प्रज्ञा जिसकी विकल,
द्विधा-कुंठित कृपाण की धार है,
परम धर्म पर टिकने की सामर्थ्य नहीं है
और न आपद्धर्म जिसे स्वीकार है।

तुझसे जो माँगते उबलते गीत अनल के,
पूछ, धर्म की वे किंचित् सीमा स्वीकार करेंगे?
मानवीय मूल्यों की जब कुछ आहुतियाँ पड़ती हों,
रोयेंगे तो नहीं? पाप से तो वे नहीं डरेंगे?

अगर कहे तू, युद्ध पुष्प, बमबाज़ी फुलझड़ियाँ हैं,
ये रोने की नहीं, मस्त, ख़ुश होने की घड़ियाँ हैं;
दाँतों से तर्जनी दबा वे चुप तो नहीं रहेंगे?
तुझ को वे दानव या दीवाना तो नहीं कहेंगे?

तब भी श्येन-धर्म ही सच है, ग़लत युद्ध में पिक है,
पूर्ण चेतना ग़लत, आज पागलपन स्वाभाविक है।

जूझ वीरता से, प्रचण्डता से, बलिष्ठ तन, मन से;
आँख मूँद कर जूझ अन्ध निर्दयता, पागलपन से।

समर पाप साकार, समर क्रीड़ा है पागलपन की,
सभी द्विधाएँ व्यर्थ समर में साध्य और साधन की।

एक वस्तु है ग्राह्य युद्ध में,
और सभी कुछ देय है;
पुण्य हो कि हो पाप,
जीत केवल दोनों का ध्येय है।

सच है, छल की विजय, अन्त तक,
विजय नहीं, अभिशाप है।
किन्तु, भूल मत, और पाप जितने घातक हों,
समर हारने से बढ़कर घातक न दूसरा पाप है।

[1962 ई.]

पाद-टिपणी

[युद्ध-काव्य की]

मेरी कविताएँ सुनकर ख़ुश होनेवाले!
तुझे ज्ञात है, इन ख़ुशियों का क्या रहस्य है?

मेरे सुख का राज़? सभ्यता के भीतर से
उठती है जो हूक, बुद्धि को विकलाती है।
कोई उत्तर नहीं। हार कर मैं मन-मारा
चौराहे पर खड़ा ज़ोर से चिल्लाता हूँ।

गर्जन धावा नहीं; स्वरों का घटाटोप है;
परित्राण का शिखर; पलायन उन प्रश्नों से
जिन का उत्तर नहीं, न कोई समाधान है।

तेरे सुख का भेद? कहीं भीतर प्राणों में
तुझ को भी काटते पाप; मन बहलाने को
तू मेरी वारुणी पान कर चिल्लाता है,

कौन पाप? है याद, उचक्के जब मंचों से
गरज रहे थे, तू ने उन्हें प्रणाम किया था?
पहनाया था उसे हार, जिसके जीवन का
कंचन है आराध्य, त्याग सूती चप्पल है।

कौन पाप? है याद, भेड़िये जब टूटे थे
तेरे घर के पास दीन-दुर्बल भेड़ों पर,
पचा गया था क्रोध सोच कर तू यह मन में
कौन विपद् में पड़े बली से वैर बढ़ा कर?

जब-जब उठा सवाल, सोचने से कतरा कर
पड़ा रहा काहिल तू इस बोदी आशा में,
कौन करे चिन्तन? खरोंच मन पर पड़ती है।
जब दस-बीस जवाब दुकानों में उतरेंगे,
हम भी लेंगे उठा एक अपनी पसन्द का।

जब चुनाव आया, तेरी आवाज़ बन्द थी;
तू शरीफ़ था, बड़ा चतुर, नीरव तटस्थ था।
जब भी दो दल लड़े, मंच से खिसक गया तू,
बड़ी बुद्धि के साथ सोच, यह कलह व्यर्थ है।
मुझ को क्या? मैं गन्धमुक्त, सब से अलिप्त हूँ।

अब समझा, चुप्पी कदर्यता की वाणी है?
बहुत अधिक चातुर्य आपदाओं का घर है।
दोषी केवल वही नहीं, जो नयनहीन था,
उस का भी है पाप, आँख थी जिसे, किन्तु, जो
बड़ी-बड़ी घड़ियों में मौन, तटस्थ रहा है।

सीधा नहीं सवाल, युद्ध घनघोर प्रश्न है!
अघी समस्त समाज, बाँध में छेद बहुत हैं।
जो सब से है अनघ, दोष कुछ उस का भी है।

कह सकता है, जो विपत्तियाँ अब आयी हैं,
तूने उनका कभी नहीं आह्वान किया था
ग़लत हुक्म कर दर्ज़ संचिकाओं पर अथवा
ग़लत ढंग से अपना घर-आँगन बुहार कर?

सरहद पर ही नहीं, मोरचे खुले हुए हैं
खेतों में, खलिहान, बैठकों, बाज़ारों में!
जहाँ कहीं आलस्य, वहीं दुर्भाग्य देश का;
जो भी नहीं सतर्क, सभी के लिए विपद् है।

और आज भी जिस पापी का सही नहीं ईमान,
(भले वह नेता हो, शासक हो या दुकानदार हो)
चीनी है, दुश्मन है, सब के लिए काल है!

कल जो किया गुनाह, आग बन कर आया है।
पर, जो हम कर रहे आज, उसका क्या होगा?
समझ नहीं नादान! पाप से छूट गये हम
सुनकर गर्जन-गीत या कि हुंकार उठाकर।

अपनी रक्षा के निमित्त औरों को रण में
कटवाना है पाप; पाप है यह विचार भी,
जगें युवक सीमा पर, हम सोने जाते हैं।

[1962 ई.]

शान्तिवादी

पुत्र मृत्यु के लिए, पिता रोने को,
माँ धुनने को सीस, वत्स आँसू पीने को,
लुटने को सिन्दूर,
उत्तराएँ विधवा होने को।

सरहद के उस पार हो कि इस पार हो,
युद्ध सोचता नहीं, कौन किसका द्रोही है।
उसका केवल ध्येय, ध्वंस हो मानवता का,
मनुज जहाँ भी हो, यम का आहार हो।

माताओं को शोक, युवतियों को विषाद है;
बेक़सूर बच्चे अनाथ होकर रोते हैं।
शान्तिवादियो! यही तुम्हारा शान्तिवाद है?

अब मत लेना नाम शान्ति का,
जिह्वा जल जायेगी,

ले-देकर जो एक शब्द है बचा, उसे भी,
तुम बकते यदि रहे,
धरित्री समझ नहीं पायेगी।
शान्तिवाद का यह नवीन सारथी तुम्हारा
नहीं शान्ति का सखा,
हलाकू है, नीरो, नमरूद है।
और उड़ाये हैं इसने उज्ज्वल कपोत जो,
उनके भीतर भरी हुई बारूद है।

[10-12-1962 ई.]

अहिंसावादी का युद्ध-गीत

हाय, मैं लिखूँ युद्ध के गीत!
बन्धु! हो गयी बड़ी अनरीत!
कण्ठ उर अन्तर के विपरीत;
देशवासी! जागो! जागो!
गांधी की रक्षा करने को गांधी से भागो!

[2]

रुधिर में रखें शीत या ताप?
अहिंसा वर है अथवा शाप?
युद्ध है पुण्य याकि दुष्पाप?
आज सारा विवाद त्यागो।
गांधी की रक्षा करने को गांधी से भागो।

[3]

सँभालें कहाँ बुद्ध का दाय?
आज छूँछे सब पिटक-निकाय।
कारगर कोई नहीं उपाय।
गिराओ बम, गोली दागो।
गांधी की रक्षा करने को गांधी से भागो।

[1962 ई.]

इतिहास का न्याय

दूर भविष्यत् के पट पर जो वाक्य लिखे हैं,
पढ़ लेना, भवितव्य अगर आगे जीवित रहने दे।

गांधी, बुद्ध, अशोक नाम हैं बड़े दिव्य स्वप्नों के।
भारत स्वयं मनुष्य-जाति की बहुत बड़ी कविता है।

कह लेना यह कथा, अगर अपनी विषाक्त डाढ़ों से
काल छोड़ दे तुझे और भवितव्य अगर कहने दे।

दर्शन की लहरें मत अधिक उछाल,
विचारों के विवर्त में पड़ा
आदमी बहुत विवश होता है।
मगरमच्छ नोचते देह का मांस और वह
छन्दों में सोचता, ऋचाओं-श्लोकों में रोता है।

दूर क्षितिज के सपने में मत भूल,
देख उस महासत्य को,
जिसकी आग प्रचण्ड, दाह दारुण, प्रत्यक्ष, विकट है।

गांधी, बुद्ध, अशोक विचारों से अब नहीं बचेंगे।
उठा खड्ग, यह और किसी पर नहीं,
स्वयं गांधी, गंगा, गौतम पर ही संकट है।

पशुता के दुर्मद झकोर में हाथ उठाकर
क्या करना आह्वान शील का, सहिष्णुता का, स्नेह का?
आत्मा की तलवार सर्वथा वहाँ व्यर्थ है,
जहाँ अखाड़ा खुला हुआ हो देह का।

द्विधा व्यर्थ, आगे का क्या इतिहास कहेगा।
द्विधा व्यर्थ, युग के चिन्तन का कहाँ ध्यान है।
दर्शन करता सदा मूक अनुसरण क्रिया का।
और जिसे हम कहते हैं इतिहास,
बड़ा ही बुद्धिमान है।

उच्च मनुजता को ठुकराने से तो वह डरता है।
किन्तु, उच्च गुण के कारण जो रण में हार गये हैं,
उन पराजितों की क़िस्मत पर रोता है इतिहास,
पर, अपाहिजों का कलंक वह क्षमा नहीं करता है।

[1962 ई.]

एनार्की

[1]

''अरे, अरे, दिन-दहाड़े ही ज़ुल्म ढाता है!
रेलवे का स्लीपर उठाये कहाँ जाता है?''

''बड़ा बेवकूफ़ है, अजब तेरा हाल है;
तुझे क्या पड़ी है? य' तो सरकारी माल है।''

''नेता या प्रणेता! तेरा ठीक तो ईमान है?
पर, दिया जाता अब देश में न ध्यान है।
बने जाते कल-कारख़ाने आलीशान भी,
साथ-साथ तेरे कुछ अपने मकान भी।''

''भाई, बकने दो उन्हें, तुम तो सुजान हो,
कविता बनाते हो, हमारे अभिमान हो।

मान लो, कभी जो चूर-धुन थोड़ा पाते हैं,
भारत से बाहर तो फेंक नहीं आते हैं।
जो भी बनवाये, अपना ही व' भवन है,
देश में ही रहता है, देश का जो धन है।''

''और, अरे यार! तू तो बड़ा शेर-दिल है,
बीच राह में ही लगा रखी महफ़िल है!
देख, लग जायें नहीं मोटर के झटके,
नाचना जो हो तो नाच सड़क से हटके।''

''सड़क से हट तू ही क्यों न चला जाता है?
मोटर में बैठ बड़ी शान दिखलाता है!
झाड़ देंगे, तुझमें जो तड़क-भड़क है,
टोकने चला है, तेरे बाप की सड़क है?

सिर तोड़ देंगे, नहीं राह से टलेंगे हम,
हाँ, हाँ, जैसे चाहें, वैसे नाच के चलेंगे हम।
बीस साल पहले की शेख़ी तुझे याद है।
भूल ही गया है, अब भारत आज़ाद है।''

[2]

सुनिए क्रोपाटकिन गोरकी!
भारत में फैली है आज़ादी बड़े ज़ोर की।
सुनता न कोई फ़रियाद है।
देखिए जिसे ही, वही ज़ोर से आज़ाद है।

लोग हैं आज़ाद बिललाने को।
नेता हैं आज़ाद जहाँ चाहें, वहाँ जाने को।
अफ़सर परम स्वतन्त्र हैं।
मन्त्रीजी हज़ार पढ़ें, लगते न मन्त्र हैं।
साहब तो खुद परीशान हैं।
चपरासी देते उन्हें पानी न तो पान हैं।

अजब हमारा यह तन्त्र है।
नक़ली दवाइयों का व्यापारी स्वतन्त्र है।
पुलिस करे जो कुछ, पाप है।
चोर का जो चाचा है, पुलिस का भी बाप है।
अख़बार मुक्त हैं चुपाने को,
विज्ञापनदाताओं का मरम छुपाने को।

और छात्र बड़े पुरज़ोर हैं।
कालिजों में सीखने को आये तोड़-फोड़ हैं।
कहते हैं, पाप है समाज में,
धिक् हम पे! जो कभी पढ़ें इस राज में।
अभी पढ़ने का क्या सवाल है?
अभी तो हमारा धर्म एक हड़ताल है।

कोई नहीं क़ैद है कपाट में,
हाट में जो आया नहीं, होगा अभी बाट में।
हाथ में हो केक या कि रोटी हो,
सूट में हो लैस या कि पहने लँगोटी हो,
कवि हो कि नेता हो कि छात्र हो,
या कि ठेला हाँकता हो, करुणा का पात्र हो;

एक बात में सभी समान हैं;
दूसरों की बात पे न देते कभी कान हैं।

हलचल बड़ी है बाज़ार में,
कोई पाँव-पैदल, चढ़ा है कोई कार में।
लेकिन, सभी की यह टेक है,
अब किसी में भी नहीं बुद्धि या विवेक है।
सरकार से न यदि ऊबेगा,
डूबेगा, अवश्य, यह सारा देश डूबेगा।

[3]

सोच-सोच आनन मलीन है,
एक ओर पाकिस्तान, एक ओर चीन है।
समझ न पड़ता चरित्र है,
रूस-अमरीका में से कौन बड़ा मित्र है।

दोस्त ही है, देख के डरो नहीं।
कम्यूनिस्ट कहते हैं, चीन से लड़ो नहीं।
चिन्तन में सोशलिस्ट गर्क़ है,
कम्यूनिस्ट और कांगरेसी में क्या फ़र्क़ है?
जनसंघी भारतीय शुद्ध हैं।
इसीलिए, आज महावीर बड़े क्रुद्ध हैं।

और कांगरेसी भी तबाह है।
ठीक-ठीक जान ही न पाता, कौन राह है।
दायाँ या कि बायाँ? कौन ठीक है?
पूछता है, यार, गांधीजी की कौन लीक है?

एक कहता है : ''चलो रूस को।''
दूसरा है चीखता कि ''मारो मनहूस को।
वाणी की स्वतन्त्रता प्रमुख है।
चुप रहने से बड़ा और कौन दुःख है?''

''तो फिर अमेरिका की बात हो?''
''लोभी, मेरे मस्तक पै भारी वज्रपात हो।
गांधीजी की बात नहीं याद है?
आदमी को यन्त्र कर देता बरबाद है।''

''तो फिर चलाएँ, चलो, तकली।''
''हम गांधीजी के भक्त होंगे नहीं नक़ली।
दबा नहीं अपने को पायेंगे;
गांधीजी के पास हरगिज नहीं जायेंगे।''

''तब तुम्हीं बोलो, हम क्या करें?''
''चाय पियें और जी में आये जो, बका करें।
बकना ही असली स्वराज है।
बाक़ी तो जहाँ भी देखो, डाकुओं का राज है।''

भोर में पुकारो सरदार को,
जीत में जो बदल देते थे कभी हार को।
तब कहो, ढोल की य' पोल है,
नेहरू के कारण ही सारा गण्डगोल है।

फिर ज़रा राजाजी का नाम लो।
याद करो जे.पी. को, विनोबा को प्रणाम दो।
तब कहो, लोहिया महान है।

एक ही तो वीर यहाँ सीना रहा तान है।

ऊपर बढ़े जो और गर्मी,
एक बारगी दो छोड़ बची-खुची नरमी।
कहो, राम! तिमिर में राह दो,
डिमोक्रेसी दूर करो, हमें तानाशाह दो।

और फिर माला ले के हाथ में
देवता से माँगो वरदान आधी रात में।
दूर रखो हमको गुनाह से,
देश को बचाये रखो राम! तानाशाह से।

क्षमा करो, क्षमा, मन्द मति है;
नेहरू को छोड़ हमें और नहीं गति है।
और जब पुन: प्रकाश हो;
बोलो, कांगरेसियो! तुम्हारा सर्वनाश हो।

[4]

जहाँ भी सुनो, वहीं आवाज़ है,
भारत में आज, बस, जीभ का स्वराज है।
और मन्त्री भी न अप्रमुख हैं।
एक कैबिनेट के अनेक यहाँ मुख हैं।

एक कहता है, हाहाकार है,
दाम पै लगाम कसो, देश की पुकार है।
दूसरे की मति अति शुद्ध है,
कहता है, नीति यह धर्म के विरुद्ध है।

गांधीजी की याद नहीं टेक है?
पूँजीपति और जनता का भाग्य एक है।
आज़ादी की धार घहराने दो,
जो भी चाहता हो, उसे छूट के कमाने दो।

[5]

चिन्तकों में अजब उमंग है।
जनता चकित और सारा विश्व दंग है।
एक कहता है, किस बात में
हम हैं स्वतन्त्र, यदि लाठी नहीं हाथ में?

घूम रहा देश किस ध्यान में,
बकरी का दूध पीके शेरों के जहान में?
वही है स्वतन्त्र, जो समर्थ है,
परमाणु-बम जो नहीं तो सब व्यर्थ है।

दूसरा है रोता, विधि वाम है;
सेनाओं का गांधीजी के देश में क्या काम है?
अहिंसा का तत्त्व यदि जानते,
हाय नेहरू जो गांधीजी को पहचानते,
सीमा पर शत्रु कोई आता क्यों?
आँखें दिखला के हमें कोई धमकाता क्यों?
भीति युद्ध-बीज सदा बोती है।
शस्त्र जहाँ रहते हैं, हिंसा वहीं होती है।

[6]

राम जाने, भीतर क्या बल है!
तब भी बखूबी यह देश रहा चल है।
गण, जन, किसी का न तन्त्र है।
साफ़ बात यह है कि भारत स्वतन्त्र है।
भिन्नता सँभाले तार-तार की,
राज करती है यहाँ चैन से 'एनार्की'।

[1962 ई.]

एक बार फिर स्वर दो-1

एक बार फिर स्वर दो।
अब भी वाणीहीन जनों की दुनिया बहुत बड़ी है।
आशा की बेटियाँ आज भी नीड़ों में सोती हैं
सुख से नहीं; विवश उड़ने के पंख नहीं होने से,
और मूक इसलिए कि उनके कण्ठ नहीं खुलते हैं।
सोचा है यह कभी कि गूँगापन कैसी पीड़ा है?
भीतर-भीतर दर्द भोगना, लेकिन, बँटा न पाना
उसे किसी से कह कर, मेरे मन को चोट लगी है।
बोल नहीं सकता जो, उसका भी दुःख कोई दुःख है?
कितने लोग समझते हैं भाषा उदास आँखों की?

एक बार फिर स्वर दो।
मूक, उदासी-भरे, दीन बेटे सम्पन्न मही के
मृत्यु-विवर के पास आज भी जीवन खोज रहे हैं।
उभर रहीं कोंपलें भेद कर सड़े हुए पत्तों को,

छाल तोड़ कर कढ़ने को टहनी छटपटा रही है।
प्रसवालय में घात लगाये खड़ी मृत्यु के मुख से
बचा नर्स भागी लेकर जिस नन्हे-से जीवन को,
देखा, वह कैसे हँसता था? मानो, समझ गया हो,
'अच्छा! यहाँ जन्म लेते ही यह सब भी होता है?'
और मृत्यु किस भाँति पराजय पर फुकार रही थी?

एक बार फिर स्वर दो।
जो अदृश्य से निकल जन्म लेने के लिए विकल हैं,
आगाही दो उन्हें, यहाँ जीवन की कनक-पुरी में
पहले दरवाज़े पर भी साँपों की कमी नहीं है;
आगे तो ये दुष्ट और भी बढ़ते ही जाते हैं।
और दुःख तो यह कि यहाँ कुछ पता नहीं करुणा का,
डँसे एक को सर्प अगर तो दस मिलकर हँसते हैं।
कहो जन्म लेनेवालों से, सोच-समझ कर आयें;
यहाँ भेड़िये गुर्राते हैं बिना किसी कारण के
या इसलिए कि हम अपना शोणित न उन्हें देते हैं।

एक बार फिर स्वर दो।
उन्हें, प्रेम-गृह में जो सपनों से प्रमत्त आये थे,
लेकिन, अब वाणिज्य देख, विस्मय से, ठमक गये हैं।
और उन्हें जो भ्रम-विनाश की चोट हृदय पर खाकर
इस गृह से चुपचाप निकल निर्जन में चले गये हैं।

एक बार फिर स्वर दो।
कहो जन्म लेनेवाले से, जिन अप्रतिम गुणों से
भेज रही है प्रकृति, बड़े नाज़ों से, उन्हें सजा कर,

सबसे पहले उन्हीं गुणों की भू पर टूट मचेगी।
वृक, शृंगाल, अहि, रँगी चोंचवाली कठोर गृध्रिणियाँ,
सब टूटेंगे एक साथ, संघर्ष भयानक होगा।
बड़ी बात होगी, इन तूफ़ानों से अगर बचा कर,
किसी भाँति अन-बुझे दीप वे वापस ले जायेंगे।

[1960 ई.]

एक बार फिर स्वर दो-2

एक बार फिर स्वर दो।
जिस गंगा के लिए भगीरथ सारी आयु तपे थे,
और हुई जो विवश छोड़ अम्बर भू पर बहने को
लाखों के आँसुओं, करोड़ों के हाहाकारों से;
लिये जा रहा इन्द्र क़ैद करने को उसे महल में।
सींचेगा वह गृहोद्यान अपना इसकी धारा से
और भगीरथ के हाथों में डण्डा थमा कहेगा,
अगर मार्क्स को मार सके तुम, हम तुमको पूजेंगे;
हार गये तो, गंगा की धारा जो ले आये हो,
उसी धार में बोर-बोर हम तुम्हें मार डालेंगे।

एक बार फिर स्वर दो।
देख रहे हो, गांधी पर कैसी विपत्ति आयी है?
तन तो उसका गया, नहीं क्या मन भी शेष बचेगा?
चुरा ले गया अगर भाव-प्रतिमा कोई मन्दिर से,

उन अपार, असहाय, बुभुक्षित लोगों का क्या होगा,
जो अब भी हैं खड़े मौन गांधी से आस लगा कर?

एक बार फिर स्वर दो।
कहो, सर्वत्यागी वह संचय का सन्तरी नहीं था,
न तो मित्र उन साँपों का जो दर्शन विरच रहे हैं
दंश मारने का अपना अधिकार बचा रखने को।

एक बार फिर स्वर दो।
उन्हें पुकारो, जो गांधी के सखा, शिष्य, सहचर हैं।
कहो, आज पावक में उनका कंचन पड़ा हुआ है।
प्रभापूर्ण होकर निकला यह तो पूज जायेगा;
मलिन हुआ तो भारत की साधना बिखर जायेगी।

एक बार फिर स्वर दो।
कहो, शान्ति का मन अशान्त है, बादल घुमर रहे हैं,
तप्त, ऊमसी हवा टहनियों में छटपटा रही है।
गांधी अगर जीत कर निकले, जलधारा बरसेगी,
हारे तो तूफ़ान इसी ऊमस से फूट पड़ेगा।

[1961 ई.]

तब भी आता हूँ मैं

टूट गये युग के दरवाज़े?
बन्द हो गई क्या भविष्य की राह?
तब भी आता हूँ मैं।

बल रहते ऐसी निर्बलता,
स्वर रहते स्वरवालों के शब्दों का अर्थाभाव!
दोपहरी में ऐसा तिमिर नहीं देखा था।

खिसक गयी शृंखला सितारों की? प्रकाश के
पुत्र वहाँ अब नहीं, जहाँ पहले उगते थे?

मही छूट सहसा विश्वम्भर के प्रबन्ध से,
सचमुच ही, पड़ गई मनुष्यों के हाथों में?

धुआँ, धुआँ सब ओर, चतुर्दिक् घुटन भरी है;
आँख मूँदने पर भी तो अब दीप्ति न आती।

तिमिर-व्यूह है ध्यान, गीत का मन काला है,
धूम-ध्वान्त फूटता कला की रेखाओं से।

तो यह सब क्या, इसी भाँति, चलता जायेगा?
यह विषपूर्ण प्रवाह? कुटिल यह घुटन प्राण की?
और वायु क्या इसी भाँति भरती जायेगी
वणिक-तुला पर चढ़ी बुद्धि के फूत्कारों से?

ना, गांधी सेठों का चौकीदार नहीं है,
न तो लौहमय छत्र जिसे तुम ओढ़ बचा लो
अपना संचित कोष मार्क्स की बौछारों से।

इस प्रकार मत पियो, आग से जल जाओगे;
गांधी शरबत नहीं, प्रखर पावक-प्रवाह था।
घोल दिया यदि इत्र कहीं अपनी शीशी का,
अनलोदक दूषित-अपेय यह हो जायेगा।

ओ विशाल तम-तोम, चतुर्दिक् घिरी घटाओ!
कब जनमेगी अशनि तुम्हारी व्याकुलता से?
धुओं और ऊमस में जो छटपटा रहा है,
वह प्रकाश कब तक खुलकर बाहर आयेगा?

दोपहरी का अन्धकार! ओ सूर्य, तुम्हारा
करने को उद्धार व्योम पर आते हैं हम,
आविष्कृत कर क्या नया प्रेम, शब्दों के भीतर
मूर्च्छित अर्थों को फिर आज जिलाते हैं हम।

पढ़ो, सामने के अक्षर क्या कहते हैं ये?
विनय विफल हो जहाँ, वाण लेना पड़ता है।
स्वेच्छा से जो न्याय नहीं देता है, उसको
एक रोज़ आख़िर सबकुछ देना पड़ता है।

टूट गये युग के दरवाज़े?
बन्द हो गयी क्या भविष्य की राह?
तब भी आता हूँ मैं।

[1960 ई.]

समर शेष है

ढीली करो धनुष की डोरी, तरकस का कस खोलो,
किसने कहा, युद्ध की वेला गई, शान्ति से बोलो?
किसने कहा, और मत बेधो हृदय वह्नि के शर से,
भरो भुवन का अंग कुंकुम से, कुसुम से, केसर से?
  कुंकुम? लेपूँ किसे? सुनाऊँ किसको कोमल गान?
  तड़प रहा आँखों के आगे भूखा हिन्दुस्तान।

फूलों की रंगीन लहर पर ओ उतरानेवाले!
ओ रेशमी नगर के वासी! ओ छवि के मतवाले!
सकल देश में हालाहल है, दिल्ली में हाला है,
दिल्ली में रौशनी, शेष भारत में अँधियाला है।
  मखमल के पर्दों के बाहर, फूलों के उस पार,
  ज्यों-का-त्यों है खड़ा आज भी मरघट-सा संसार।

वह संसार जहाँ पर पहुँची अब तक नहीं किरण है,
जहाँ क्षितिज है शून्य, अभी तक अम्बर तिमिर-वरण है।
देख जहाँ का दृश्य आज भी अन्तस्तल हिलता है,
माँ को लज्जा-वसन और शिशु को न क्षीर मिलता है।
पूछ रहा है जहाँ चकित हो जन-जन देख अकाज,
सात वर्ष हो गये, राह में अटका कहाँ स्वराज?

अटका कहाँ स्वराज? बोल दिल्ली! तू क्या कहती है?
तू रानी बन गई, वेदना जनता क्यों सहती है?
सबके भाग दबा रक्खे हैं किसने अपने कर में?
उतरी थी जो विभा, हुई वन्दिनी, बता, किस घर में?
समर शेष है, यह प्रकाश बन्दी-गृह से छूटेगा,
और नहीं तो तुझ पर पापिनि! महावज्र टूटेगा।

समर शेष है, इस स्वराज्य को सत्य बनाना होगा।
जिसका है यह न्यास, उसे सत्वर पहुँचाना होगा।
धारा के मग में अनेक पर्वत जो खड़े हुए हैं,
गंगा का पथ रोक इन्द्र के गज जो अड़े हुए हैं,
कह दो उनसे, झुके अगर तो जग में यश पायेंगे,
अड़े रहे तो ऐरावत पत्तों-से बह जायेंगे।

समर शेष है, जनगंगा को खुलकर लहराने दो,
शिखरों को डूबने और मुकुटों को बह जाने दो।
पथरीली, ऊँची ज़मीन है? तो उसको तोड़ेंगे।
समतल पीटे बिना समर की भूमि नहीं छोड़ेंगे।
समर शेष है, चलो ज्योतियों के बरसाते तीर,
खण्ड-खण्ड हो गिरे विषमता की काली ज़ंजीर।

समर शेष है, अभी मनुज-भक्षी हुंकार रहे हैं।
गांधी का पी रुधिर, जवाहर पर फुँकार रहे हैं।
समर शेष है, अहंकार इनका हरना बाक़ी है,
वृक को दन्तहीन, अहि को निर्विष करना बक़ी है।
समर शेष है, शपथ धर्म की, लाना है वह काल,
विचरें अभय देश में गांधी और जवाहरलाल।[1]

तिमिर-पुत्र ये दस्यु कहीं कोई दुष्कांड रचें ना!
सावधान, हो खड़ी देश भर में गांधी की सेना।
बलि देकर भी बली! स्नेह का यह मृदु व्रत साधो रे!
मन्दिर औ' मस्जिद, दोनों पर एक तार बाँधो रे!
समर शेष है, नहीं पाप का भागी केवल व्याध,
जो तटस्थ हैं, समय लिखेगा उनका भी अपराध।

[1953 ई.]

1. जवाहरलाल नेहरू पर एक व्यक्ति ने छुरा चलाने की कोशिश की थी।

जवानी का झण्डा

घटा फाड़कर जगमगाता हुआ
आ गया देख, ज्वाला का बाण;
खड़ा हो, जवानी का झण्डा उड़ा,
ओ मेरे देश के नौजवान!

[1]

सहम करके चुप हो गये थे समुन्दर
अभी सुन के तेरी दहाड़;
ज़मीं हिल रही थी, जहाँ हिल रहा था,
अभी हिल रहे थे पहाड़;
अभी क्या हुआ? किसके जादू ने आ करके
शेरों की सी दी ज़ुबान?
खड़ा हो, जवानी का झण्डा उड़ा,
ओ मेरे देश के नौजवान!

[2]

खड़ा हो कि पच्छिम के कुचले हुए लोग
उठने लगे ले मशाल,
खड़ा हो कि पूरब की छाती से भी
फूटने को है ज्वाला कराल!
खड़ा हो कि फिर फूँक विष की लगा
धूर्जटी ने बजाया विषान,
खड़ा हो, जवानी का झण्डा उड़ा,
ओ मेरे देश के नौजवान!

[3]

गरज कर बता सबको, मारे किसी के
मरेगा नहीं हिन्द-देश,
लहू की नदी तैर कर आ रहा है,
कहीं से कहीं हिन्द-देश।
लड़ाई के मैदान में चल रहे लेके
हम उसका उड़ता निशान,
खड़ा हो, जवानी का झण्डा उडा,
ओ मेरे देश के नौजवान!

[4]

अहा! जगमगाने लगी रात की
माँग में रौशनी की लकीर,
अहा! फूल हँसने लगे, सामने देख,
उड़ने लगा वह अबीर।

अहा! यह उषा हो के उड़ता चला
आ रहा देवता का विमान;
खड़ा हो, जवानी का झण्डा उड़ा,
ओ मेरे देश के नौजवान!

●●●